CW01281465

A Family at War
1914-1918

A Family at War
1914-1918

The Family of
Mr & Mrs Charles Brown Stout MPS
of the Medical Hall, Lerwick, Shetland Islands

MARGARET STUART

A Family at War 1914-1918

First published by The Shetland Times Ltd., 2021.
ISBN 978-1-910997-36-9

Copyright © Margaret Stuart, 2021.

All rights reserved.
No part of this publication may be reproduced, stored in a retrieval system or transmitted, in any form, by any means, electronic, mechanical, photocopying, recording or otherwise without the prior written consent of the publishers.

A catalogue record for this book is available from the British Library.
British Library Cataloguing-in-Publication Data

Printed and published by
The Shetland Times Ltd.,
Gremista, Lerwick,
Shetland ZE1 0PX.

To my uncle, Charlie Stout, whose precious photographic albums are the inspiration for this book.

Contents

Author's Note ix
Family Tree x
Acknowledgements xi
Introduction xiii
Family Life Before 1914 1
Greig's Closs 3
Charles Brown Stout MPS 1845-1928 11
Margaret Mainland Stout 1859-1946 23
Anne Elizabeth Stout 1887-1976 35
Elizabeth Brown Stout 1890-1973 67
Francisca Mary Stout 1890-1913 89
Charles Brown Stout 1891-1974 91
Margaret Bannatyne Stout 1894-1982 121
James Stout 1898-1953 151
Harriet Mainland Stout 1896-1984 165
Jessie Alexandra Stout 1901-1982 175
Captain Henry Mainland 1876-1932 181
The Cousins Who Went to War 187
Appendix 195
Bibliography 204

The Fish Mart, Lerwick 1913

Author's Note

Mr and Mrs Charles Brown Stout and Family of the Shetland Islands.

I had been sharing the photographic archive I had inherited from my uncle, Charles Brown Stout MPS of the Medical Hall Pharmacy Lerwick, with Dr Ian Tait, curator of the Shetland Museum. Charles Stout had bought his first cameras in 1910 and recorded family life and events in Shetland over the next 30 years. I mentioned to Dr Tait that I was thinking of publishing a book of Charles Stout's photographs showing a unique aspect of life in Shetland at that time.

The commemoration of the centenary of the First World War had just begun, "why not a Family at War?" suggested Dr Tait, and so the idea took root. Charles Stout's photographic archive is the inspiration for this book and the connecting thread throughout the story. I also inherited from my mother, Margaret Stout, a large archive of written material and ephemera, and my cousin Isobel Irvine shared precious war diaries which had belonged to her grandmother, Anne Stout.

The book is a testimony to the life of an aspiring Shetland family, before, during and just after the First World War. Each member of the family supported the war in their own way, in Shetland, in London and in France, during the war and after the armistice. They accepted that their country was threatened and without question gave their all. For four of them the war changed the course of their lives forever.

The sisters were prodigious correspondents and letters were circulated around the family, diaries kept, articles written for publication and lectures prepared. Compiling this book with so much diverse information has been a huge but rewarding task. I have recorded the facts and their thoughts as I found them. For me it has been a privilege to get to know my grandparents, my mother, and my aunts and uncles all over again at this auspicious time in their lives.

I hope I have been faithful to their ideals, and that readers will enter into the spirit of their book.

Margaret Stuart.

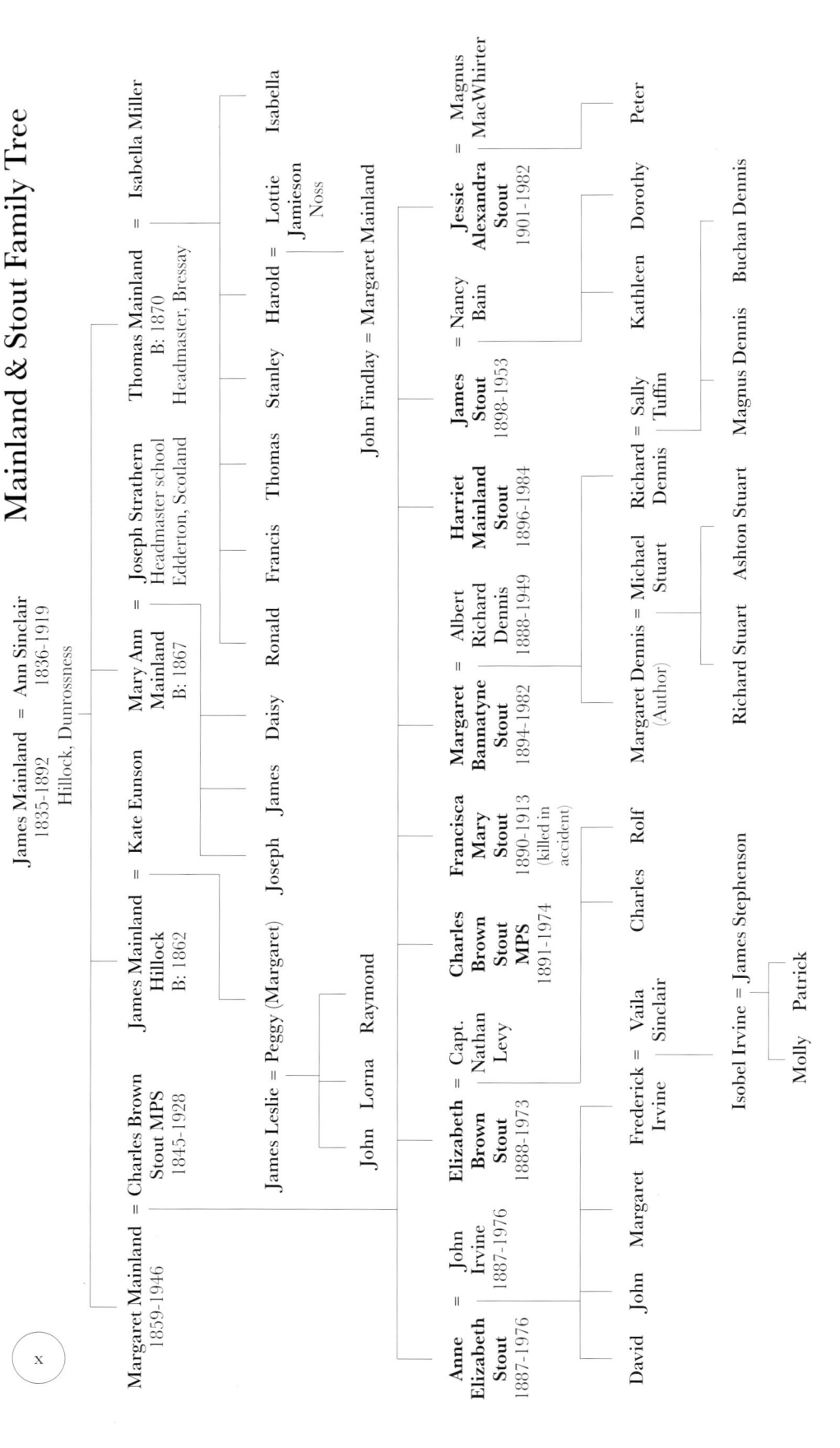

Mainland & Stout Family Tree

James Mainland = Ann Sinclair
1835-1892   1836-1919
Hillock, Dumrossness

- Margaret Mainland = Charles Brown Stout MPS
  1859-1946   1845-1928
- James Mainland
  Hillock
  B: 1862
  = Kate Eunson
- Mary Ann Mainland
  B: 1867
  = Joseph Strathern
  Headmaster school
  Edderton, Scotland
- Thomas Mainland
  B: 1870
  Headmaster, Bressay
  = Isabella Miller

Children of Mary Ann & Joseph Strathern: Joseph, James, Daisy, Ronald, Francis, Thomas, Stanley, Harold = Lottie Jamieson Noss, Isabella

John Findlay = Margaret Mainland

Children of Margaret Mainland & Charles Brown Stout:
- James Leslie = Peggy (Margaret) — children: John, Lorna, Raymond
- Anne Elizabeth Stout 1887-1976 = John Irvine 1887-1976
- Elizabeth Brown Stout 1888-1973 = Capt. Nathan Levy
- Francisca Mary Stout 1890-1913 (killed in accident)
- Charles Brown Stout MPS 1891-1974 — Charles, Rolf
- Margaret Bannatyne Stout 1894-1982 = Albert Richard Dennis 1888-1949
- Harriet Mainland Stout 1896-1984
- James Stout 1898-1953 = Nancy Bain
- Jessie Alexandra Stout 1901-1982 = Magnus MacWhirter — Peter

Children of Anne Elizabeth Stout & John Irvine:
- David, John, Margaret, Frederick = Vaila Sinclair, Isobel Irvine = James Stephenson — Molly, Patrick

Children of Margaret Bannatyne Stout & Albert Richard Dennis:
- Margaret Dennis (Author) = Michael Stuart — Richard Stuart, Ashton Stuart
- Magnus Dennis
- Richard Dennis = Sally Tuffin
- Kathleen
- Dorothy
- Buchan Dennis

x

Acknowledgements

I would like to thank Davy Cooper, Margaret Findlay, Professor John Gooch, Linda Gowans, The Imperial War Museum, Angus Johnson, Graham Johnston, Jeremy Mitchell, Richard Stuart, Brian Smith (Archivist Shetland Museum and Archives), the staff of the Shetland Library, Ashton Stuart, Jon Sandison, Brian Stout, Dr Ian Tait (Curator Shetland Museum and Archives) and Dr Jonathan Wills for sharing their knowledge and enthusiasm for the book, and for their encouragement and technical expertise.

A special thank you to Isobel Irvine for sharing her grandmother's war diaries and photographs, the family cuttings book and Medical Hall Visitors' book.

I would also like to thank Charlotte Black and Iain Currie of The Shetland Times Ltd for their patience and professionalism in seeing the project through.

I owe a dept of gratitude to Davy Cooper for his technical help in reproducing the photographs for this book. I also asked him for his opinion on the first script of the book and his comments spurred me on. I am so sad that Davy died before publication and that I cannot give him a copy of the book as planned.

Hello Margaret

Unfortunately I haven't had time to do much more than skim through the book. It is a testament to its "readability" that I had to stop myself becoming too immersed with the various members of the Stout family. What a fastinating and unconventional bunch!!

I think this will make a great publication and give a very different perspective on the period.

Cheers

Davy.

Margaret Stuart,
2021.

Griegs Closs and back door to the Medical Hall. The upper floor of the lodberrie was tenanted by Mrs Williamson and her son
Photograph by J.D.Rattar Courtesy of the Shetland Museum and Archives

Introduction

Mr and Mrs Charles Brown Stout and Family
The Shetland Islands 1914

More than one hundred years have passed since the start of the First World War, yet our awareness has not diminished, if anything it has been strengthened as information technology has given us access to countless war records. Our own family archives, precious social documents, are a connecting thread for ordinary people to those momentous times.

This is the story of an aspiring Shetland family and their contribution to the social history of the First World War.

The Medical Hall, 92 Commercial Street, Lerwick, was the pharmacy, chemist shop and home to Charles Brown Stout MPS and his wife Margaret Mainland Stout, and was at the heart of a bustling family life.

Their eight children were born there between 1887 and 1901. They were educated at the Anderson Educational Institute in Lerwick, and continued their education at college and university in Edinburgh and Glasgow.

They were all of an age and background that allowed them some choice in the way they responded to the war.

Young men, like James Stout, raced to enlist in case they missed out in the great adventure. Young women left the security of home, as the Stout girls did, to do "their bit".

For four of them the war changed their lives forever.

The German warship *Hansa*, 1904.

The Esplanade and sailing ship *Ariel* from Victoria Pier, 1913.

Family Life Before 1914

Although remote, the Shetland Islands were at the centre of a maritime cross, facilitating trading opportunities and cultural exchanges.

Lerwick, the capital, was a cosmopolitan town and the family were accustomed, as were most Shetlanders, to meeting foreigners. Dr Van Asperen of the Dutch hospital ship *De Hoop*, which lay in Bressay Sound while the Dutch fleet fished in the waters around Shetland, became a family friend. His daughters corresponded with the Stout girls and later they exchanged visits.

On Sundays the girls were encouraged to paint watercolours. The constantly changing view of the harbour from the drawing room windows provided inspiration in all weathers. Or, encouraged by Mama, they wrote letters to their cousins in Australia, several of whom enlisted and were posted to the Western Front. A few spent their leave with the family in Shetland and Charlie recorded their visits on camera.

There must have been some confusion in the minds of Shetlanders when they read the news, "Britain Declares War Against Germany".

In 1904 the family would have seen from their windows the German Fleet anchored in Bressay Sound and, as recently as June 1914, the 31 German fishing vessels leaving Lerwick. Germany had provided the main route for the export of the islands' staple product, salt herring. Shetland and German fish merchants worked closely together and had formed business friendships. Now, suddenly, Germany had become the arch enemy!

Given this conflicting evidence, it is understandable that Shetlanders received the news of war with mixed emotions. *The Shetland News* trumpeted headlines, "KEEN ENTHUSIASM ALL OVER SHETLAND" "INITIAL EXCITEMENT" "THE WOMEN FELT ANXIETY AND UNCERTAINTY" "OVERALL CALMNESS AND FORTITUDE".

Patriotic zeal engulfed the family sending James, underage, hurrying to enlist, and Mrs Stout and her daughters to immerse themselves in war work. For the four eldest girls, already embarked on careers, the war provided untold opportunities to broaden their horizons.

This narrative is a compilation from family diaries, letters and conversations, and illustrated with family photographs by the young Charles Brown Stout who purchased his first professional camera in 1910.

In 1904 thirty warships of the German Fleet homeward bound from a review in Plymouth, paid a visit to Lerwick Harbour. Germany had built up a large naval fleet to challenge British supremacy at sea, and had become aware of Shetland's strategic location. The German fleet was met with enthusiasm and hospitality, several ships opened to the public, who enjoyed searchlight and firework displays. Social gatherings and a football match were organised. But there was an underlying unease and the request to stage a night attack on Lerwick was quickly refused.

A catch of fish on the Esplanade.

Greig's Closs

The Medical Hall and Lodberrie, built in 1798, was the town house of the Greigs of Leog. The pharmacy and chemist shop were converted from part of the ground floor at a later date. The building extending from the back of the house and into the sea was called a lodberrie and was used to store goods brought in by boat. In earlier days fishing boats would smuggle goods from Holland into Lerwick via the lodberrie. The old house abounded with cubby holes where Dutch gin and tobacco could be safely hidden. Years after the esplanade was built an old iron boat ring could still be seen in the lodberrie wall.

The photograph of Greig's Closs (see photograph opposite the introduction page), the lane leading from the sea to the back door of the Medical Hall, was taken by J.D. Rattar, a Shetlander and noted landscape photographer.

The stone bridge spanning Greig's Closs led to the upper floor of the lodberrie which was tenanted by a Barbara Williamson and her son. Fair Isle knitwear was in great demand after the Prince of Wales wore a Fair Isle jumper playing golf at St Andrews in 1922. Accomplished knitters, like Barbara Williamson, were quick to learn the new patterns and to make Fair Isle garments in the fashionable style for a ready market. Her Fair Isle jumper has been washed and is now drying on a jumper board ready to be sold, possibly to Schoor Muir & Co. a retail knitwear business nearby, who unusually paid in cash for their knitwear instead of the inequitable truck (barter) system.

Other rooms in the lodberrie were let to a woman who catered for wedding parties. It had become fashionable for country couples to be married in Lerwick, and she provided the room and refreshments for the nuptials. The Stout girls were never allowed to attend these celebrations, but young Charlie, undetected, used to slip in. He said they were very merry and the wedding cake and refreshments were placed for safety in the box bed!

For Charlie, the unassuming back door became the backdrop for countless photographs of family and friends. The area around the back door provided the only private area of daylight outside the house. Charlie, determined to leave his mark, carved a large C.S. into the stone wall.

Mr Stout closed the access from the Closs to the Street and built a large entrance hall to the house opening onto the Street. The 18th century front door with the beautiful fanlight was now inside the house. The property also extended to a wide

A Family at War

strip of ground to the right of the lodberrie. Matty, who had a fish stall on the Esplanade, came to Mr and Mrs Stout in great distress. She had lost her site and with it her livelihood. Would they allow her to put up her fish stall alongside the lodberrie until she could find another site? They agreed, providing she found a permanent site soon, which she did. In the meantime, the family received an unexpected supply of fresh fish!

James Rattar's iconic photograph of Greig's Closs has assured it a place in history.

Lerwick before the building of the Esplanade in 1883.
The lodberries can clearly be seen extending into the sea.
Photograph by George Washington Wilson.

Lerwick Harbour. The new esplanade was completed in 1886.
The Medical Hall lodberrie (2nd from right) no longer extends into the sea.

Portrait of Mr C. B. Stout MPS on his wedding day in Edinburgh, 6th October, 1886.

Charles Brown Stout MPS 1845-1928

The Years Before the War

Charles Brown Stout was 69 years old in 1914. In 1863 aged eighteen he had arrived in Lerwick from his home in the island of Unst, to start his apprenticeship with Dr Petrus Dorotheus Loeterbagh, a Dutch doctor, who had established a medical practice and pharmacy in Lerwick known as the Medical Hall.

Young Charles Stout had received some tuition in Latin from the schoolmaster at Uyeasound, and realised that Latin was the key to academic success.

A traveller arrived in Uyeasound on his way to Baltasound, 10 miles distant, and asked Charles if he would accompany him and carry his bag. Charles agreed, and on reaching Baltasound the traveller gave Charles one shilling and six pence which Charles joyously spent on a Latin grammar book. Dr Spence, who lived on the Isle of Uyea, had engaged a tutor for his son and invited Charles to study with him, both boys intent on a career in medicine. Charles was overjoyed at his good fortune and the two boys worked well together, rivals and friends. Charles studied grammar, learnt to write a beautiful copperplate hand, and to speak "correctly". Charles blossomed, and aged 18 he was ready to start his apprenticeship with Dr Loeterbagh in Lerwick.

Charles was a diligent and companionable apprentice and he and Dr Loeterbagh worked well together. On 2nd April, 1867, when word reached Lerwick that the whaling ship *Diana*,[1] given up for lost to the Arctic winter, had been sighted off Ronas Voe, Dr Loeterbagh and Charles rode north together to meet the stricken ship and give medical help to the survivors.

Dr Loeterbagh introduced Charles to the Freemasons when he arrived in Lerwick as a young man, and he became a member of the Lerwick Lodge for the rest of his

---

1   The Whaling ship *Diana* became frozen in ice while on a whaling expedition to Baffin Bay in 1867. The captain and several members of the crew died. They had set sail with two month's provisions and eleven months later they finally reached Ronas Voe, North Mainland, Shetland. The surviving crew were in need of immediate medical care.

life. Unfortunately in 1871 Dr Loeterbagh contracted smallpox from a Dutch sailor and died. Charles Stout took over the management of the pharmacy until 1878 when he purchased the Medical Hall, house, shop and business. He was now a qualified pharmacist and also had a licence to practice dentistry, but he was unable to continue his medical apprenticeship. He may not have had the medical qualifications that he hoped for but he was expected to treat the customers who came to the shop with all manner of ailments. To consult one of the few doctors was considerably more expensive.

Minor surgery often had to be performed. The removal of large barbed fish hooks embedded in leathery skin was routine. The largest and strongest patients were usually the first to faint at the sight of their own blood, allowing Mr Stout to perform the "surgery" in peace. Removing fish scales from eyes was a tricky but common occurrence.

All work and no play, makes Jack a dull boy! Charles Stout took holidays in Scotland and England, and with his cousin Archie Sutherland he took a Victorian gentleman's cruise on the Rhine.

In 1886 he married Margaret Mainland from the Hillock, Dunrossness, in Anderson's Private Hotel, Melville Street, Edinburgh. They spent some time in Edinburgh before travelling home to Shetland by steamer. On reaching Lerwick they came ashore in a small boat to the steps below the Medical Hall lodberrie. They walked up the closs to the front door on Commercial Street and up the beautiful curving stone staircase to the drawing room where family and friends were waiting to greet the new Mrs Stout.

Mr Stout met many interesting visitors to Shetland who came into the shop, including the Dutchess of Bedford whose yacht *Sapphire* anchored in Bressay Sound while waiting for good weather to sail to Fair Isle. She rented a small cottage on Fair Isle where she stayed alone with her maid and pursued her passion for ornithology. She once accepted an invitation to take tea and Mrs Stout remarked afterwards, "and it was just a cup of tea". When war broke out in 1914 she offered to place herself, her crew and her yacht at the disposal of the Admiralty. The offer was declined.

Charles' daughter Margaret writes of her father:

> He was quite a sport. He must have shot at one time because there was a row of stuffed birds on top of the bookcase. I always liked the Great Northern Diver best. He kept a boat for rowing to Bressay where he played golf and visited his brother in law, Thomas Mainland who was the headmaster of the Bressay School. In summer he played bowls on the town green and golf on the Knab, and if it was a severe winter, he took his curling stone and joined friends on Clickamin Loch. He enjoyed a game of cards, and when homework was done, would suggest a game of whist to relax everyone before bed.

Mr Stout and Dr Van Asperen of the Dutch hospital ship *De Hoop* had become good friends. *De Hoop* lay moored in Bressay Sound below the Medical Hall and in the evening he enjoyed smoking a good Dutch cigar with the doctor. Occasionally he was lured out on a family expedition, and photographs show a rather stiff elderly gentleman looking steadfastly away from the camera.

In 1913 his daughter Betty proposed keeping a visitors' book in the Medical Hall, and with the family in agreement she purchased a book, and on 1st September, 1913, all the family signed in order of seniority. One of the first visitors to sign the book was Jessie M.E. Saxby, the Shetland author, and her daughter Lorna Maud Saxby, followed by George Ramsay the photographer, Captain and Mrs Anderson, and a host of friends and relations from all over Shetland and beyond. The book gives an unprecedented insight into everyday life at the Medical Hall.

Mr Stout was a member of the Lerwick Club which rented rooms in the Town Hall, where the members played billiards, cards, cribbage and yarned. He was a Mason, a member of the Lerwick Lodge, and his property entitled him to membership of the Feuars and Heritors. For some years he was a member of the Zetland County Council where his opinions and quiet reasoned judgement were sought and respected. Local politics were dominated by a tightly knit group of Lerwick based businessmen.

His daughter Margaret said of him, "Papa was a gentle kindly man and never raised his voice to any of us or punished us, and we would never have done anything to displease him."

The Dutchess of Bedford's steam yacht the *Sapphire* anchored in Lerwick harbour. Charlie's motor boat is moored in the foreground.

The Lerwick esplanade. The Medical Hall and lodberrie, 1884, are marked with a cross.

Mr Stout and Gilbert Johnston RNVR, an old friend from Unst. The Isle of Noss in the background.

Charles Brown Stout MPS 1845-1928

The War Years

Lerwick was a bustling town during the war years and business in the Medical Hall was good. Just as well. Mr Stout was something of a philanthropist. He took it upon himself to educate, feed and clothe three nephews. Each had lost a parent through bereavement. Two qualified as chemists after serving their apprenticeships in the Medical Hall and established businesses in Glasgow and Montreal. The other became a civil servant in Vancouver. At the start of the war they all enlisted and returned to Shetland on leave.

There was always an apprentice in the shop, which was open until 9 o'clock at night when the apprentice went home, but often Mr Stout would still be dispensing at midnight! All the powders were weighed and measured on a square of white paper and folded over a machine to a standard size. Cough mixtures and tonics were made in large quantities and bottles filled and labelled. These were more profitable than selling the proliferation of patent medicines. Pills were made by compounding ingredients into a pliable mass with a pestle and mortar. The mixture was then rolled on a board before being cut by the pill machine and rolled by hand into small pills to be rolled in chalk for insurance prescriptions, varnish for paying customers, and a gold or silver finish for those who could afford them. All very labour intensive. No wonder Mr Stout was still dispensing at midnight.

Every prescription was numbered and entered into a large book and a separate poisons register faithfully kept, revealing to our eyes an extraordinary casual use of what are now prohibited drugs unless prescribed by a doctor. An effective cough mixture was the Elixir of Heroin containing chiefly heroin but no customer, to their knowledge, ever became an addict. An artistic apprentice with a sense of humour painted a skull and crossbones on one door of the poison cupboard and a self portrait on the other door!

Mr Stout was an old fashioned pharmacist who mixed his own medicines, rolled his own pills and people consulted him as they would a doctor. Mr Blance the baker was distraught, his baby son was critically ill. The doctor had given up all hope. Mr

Blance begged Mr Stout to do something. He consulted an old book of prescriptions belonging to Dr Loeterbagh and prepared a remedy which included laudanum. The baby recovered and the Stout family got a Christmas cake every year!

People wrote to Mr Stout from all over Shetland seeking medical advice and cures and he no doubt did his best to reply. I would love to know what his response was to a very thin lady who wrote an anguished letter desperate to become plump and attract a husband. And the crofter who returned the large pills prescribed with a note "that it would take the stomach of a horse to digest them".

Dentistry was mostly confined to extractions. A rigid chair was installed in the back room of the shop, to constrain the patient and give the dentist maximum room to manoeuvre. The blood-curdling roars from the unfortunate having a molar extracted could be heard throughout the house. The one shilling charge was popped into a tin towards a new piano!

Mr Stout must have been relieved when his eldest son Charlie, now a qualified pharmacist, took on the responsibility of the business in 1914. He quietly took a back seat as Charlie propelled the business into the 20th century. He had difficulty persuading himself that photography, cosmetics and hair products had a place in a pharmacy, but as the business continued to prosper, he kept his thoughts to himself.

The chemist shop was very busy during the war years and Mr Stout enjoyed meeting the servicemen who frequented the shop. The convoy system was instituted in 1917 and Lerwick became the allies' convoy port. Lerwick harbour was filled with ships and the streets with men in uniform. Many found their way to the home of the hospitable Mr and Mrs Stout and this is reflected in the astonishing number of servicemen and shipwrecked foreigners who recorded their names in the Medical Hall Visitor Book. During 1917, 4,500 vessels passed through Bressay Sound, greater than any other port in the kingdom. No wonder that 223 servicemen and shipwrecked foreigners are recorded in the Medical Hall visitors' book for 1917.

Lieut. Frank Johnson RNVR, Lieut. L.R. Robson RNR nicknamed "The Pirate", and Lieut. R. Watson RNVR, who were billeted across the street from the Medical Hall in the Grand Hotel, became family friends. The Medical Hall soon became a second home to them and their friends. They joined in Christmas and New Year festivities and even went out guizing with the younger members of the family when the war was drawing to a close.

Many of the naval personnel not only signed the visitor book but also gave the name of their ship. The blockade ships of Basta Voe sent neutral ships under escort to the depot and guard ship HMS *Brilliant*, which was stationed in Lerwick harbour. Mr and Mrs Stout welcomed Mr Cullin the chaplin on the *Brilliant*, to their home, and introduced him to several Shetland ministers.

The drifter HMT *Ruby Gem*, converted by the admiralty to a naval craft and armed with guns, patrolled the coast of Shetland searching for submarines. Two members of the crew, Leonard Ballett and William Mouat, a Shetlander, made several visits to the house at Mr Stout's invitation.

On 2nd August, 1918, Lieut. Drewry VC was accidentally killed while on Northern Patrol. The funeral held in Lerwick was impressive. The coffin was mounted on a gun carriage and the route was lined with hundreds of naval personnel. When the funeral was over Mr Stout invited several of them to the house for refreshment. Their names are recorded in the visitor book on that sad day.

Commander W.E. Smith had Shetland connections and regarded the Medical Hall as his second home. He makes his first visit in March 1916 and his name appears regularly in the visitors' book until the end of the war. Commander W.E. Smith DSO RD RNVR had a distinguished war record; he was captain of HMS *President* in 1915, commander of HMS *Duke of Cornwall* in 1916, commander of HMS *Rosebell* in 1917 and Commodore of Convoy in 1918. He invited all the family to visit him in Southampton. Several of them did, and you can read Margaret's account of her visit in 1918 later in the book.

I am curious about so many other visitors. Seier Gh Jonesco 2nd engineer and Virgil Nariod 1st mate of the SS *Bucuristi*. And who was Monsirur Corbusier from Liege? It is heartening to see Shetland friends home on leave among all these strangers. A.M. Frank Anderson RAF, A.S. Reid Tait RNVR, Pte Ronnie Mathewson and Lieut. Harry Kay, Lerwick. L'Cpl. James Smith and Gilbert Johnston RNVR, Unst. Pte. Tom Mainland RAF, Bressay, and Lance Cpl. W. Sandison, Lerwick, to name a few.

James Stout returned home on 28th December, 1917, after being wounded twice at the Battle of Arras and spending eight months in hospital in Woolwich. "Kill the fatted calf" exclaims the visitors' book!

On the 27th October, 1917, the Romanian merchant ship SS *Juil*, sailing from Archangelsk to Shetland to join a convoy to England, ran onto rocks in Braewick, Lerwick. Passengers and crew were all evacuated safely to dry land, and the ship was salvaged by J.W. Robertson and taken to his yard in Lerwick to undergo extensive repairs. The SS *Juil* would not be ready to sail again until 18th January, 1918.

Mr Stout's daughter Anne spent all her spare time at the Scottish Church Army Hut at Alexandra Wharf, Lerwick, a social club for servicemen. The hut was also used as a distribution centre for food and clothing for men and women rescued from Shetland waters. The army hut became the first port of call for the shipwrecked Romanians from the SS *Juil* and Anne assisted in finding them accommodation in Lerwick. And an invitation to the Medical Hall.

Several of them including Captain Stefan Christesco took up residence in the Grand Hotel and it was not long before Lieut. Frank Johnson RNVR and Lieut.

A Family at War

Lawrence Robson RNR introduced them to Mr and Mrs Stout. Inscribed in the margin of the visitor book on the 27th October; "SS *Juil* on rocks at Lerwick" and on that very day six survivors called at the Medical Hall. Le Capitaine Stefan Christesco, Paulinea Balteanu, T.Balteanu, Elizabetha Balteanu, J. Dimitrise (Chief Officer) and Victor Sviskry (2nd Engineer). The crew and passengers were delighted to meet the hospitable Mr and Mrs Stout and their family and became frequent visitors over the next two months. Margaret's diary takes up the story:

> Captain Christesco was a Romanian architect who had escaped from Romania leaving his wife and daughters with the Germans. When Le Capitaine Christesco came into the drawing room he announced, "Ahh! I like this, it is a home. I will come every day!" And he did until the ship was ready to sail again. He had written books on Relativity in opposition to Einstein, in French, which he spoke fluently. He gave two signed copies to Anne who also spoke fluent French.

On 3rd November two other shipwrecked Romanians visited the Medical Hall, Michel Cocias and N. Foachisru, followed closely by N. Joachim (1st Engineer) and the original six visitors. Then, Monsieurs – Joashim, Svesky, Dimicrieu, Davidisco and Cocia, passengers on the SS *Juil* added their names to the book and Le Captaine Christesco pops up all the time as he said he would. A party of Romanians helped to see in the New Year and then on the 3rd and 5th January they called to make their farewells. The SS *Juil* was ready to sail. We meet Le Capitaine Christesco again in London where he calls on Margaret Stout.

Mr and Mrs Stout welcomed servicemen and shipwrecked foreigners into their home and were generous with their hospitality. Instinctively they were contributing to the war effort in the way they knew best. And what a wonderful contribution![1]

Mr Stout must have discussed the war with his friends at the Town Hall, but what his personal thoughts were I do not know. He was never an effusive man, and I think, his thoughts were quietly philosophical about the war. He was always supportive of the time-consuming war work undertaken by his wife and he was pleased to be asked to act as master of ceremonies at wartime fundraising events. He did not discourage his daughters and son from enlisting their services to the war effort, and I know that he was proud of their achievements. But he must have been concerned for James in France, Betty in Paris, Margaret in London and Anne in Cologne. He felt deeply for his friend Thomas Manson whose son Karl was killed in the same battle his own son

---

1   1916-67 servicemen received hospitality in the Medical Hall.
    1917-1918. 223 servicemen including Romanian refugees received hospitality in the Medical Hall.

James, was wounded and Henry Mainland in Australia, whose only son Henry O. Mainland, was killed in Belgium before he had leave to visit the family in Shetland. His three Australian nephews were wounded, one at Galipoli and two in France. At the beginning of the war Mr and Mrs Stout's third daughter, Francisca Mary aged 23 years was accidentally killed in a cycling accident on her way home from the Cunningsburgh School where she was a teacher. This was a greater tragedy to them than the war. Mr Stout wrote in his diary, "This is the saddest day of my life."

The Mainland family on Bressay had their own cross to bear. On 1st June, 1917, their fourteen-year-old son Ronald Sinclair Mainland was accidentally killed in a fall from the cliffs beyond the lighthouse. He trod on a projecting stone which had been used as a stepping stone for generations; it gave way plunging Ronald to his death. The loss of this young life was mourned throughout Shetland.

The war over, life moved on slowly for Mr Stout now that Charlie was successfully managing the business. He had time for leisurely sporting activities and a daily visit to the shop to chat with old friends.

Mr Stout enjoyed the company of the young people who gathered in the Medical Hall, and would occasionally accompany them on picnics or make a guest appearance at the many parties held in the old dining room.

The letters that poured into the Medical Hall when he died are testament to the love and respect in which he was held by people all over Shetland.

The inauguration of the Medical Hall Visitors' Book, September 1913.

Three pages from the Medical Hall visitors' book 1917, witness to the extraordinary number of servicemen who visited the Medical Hall.

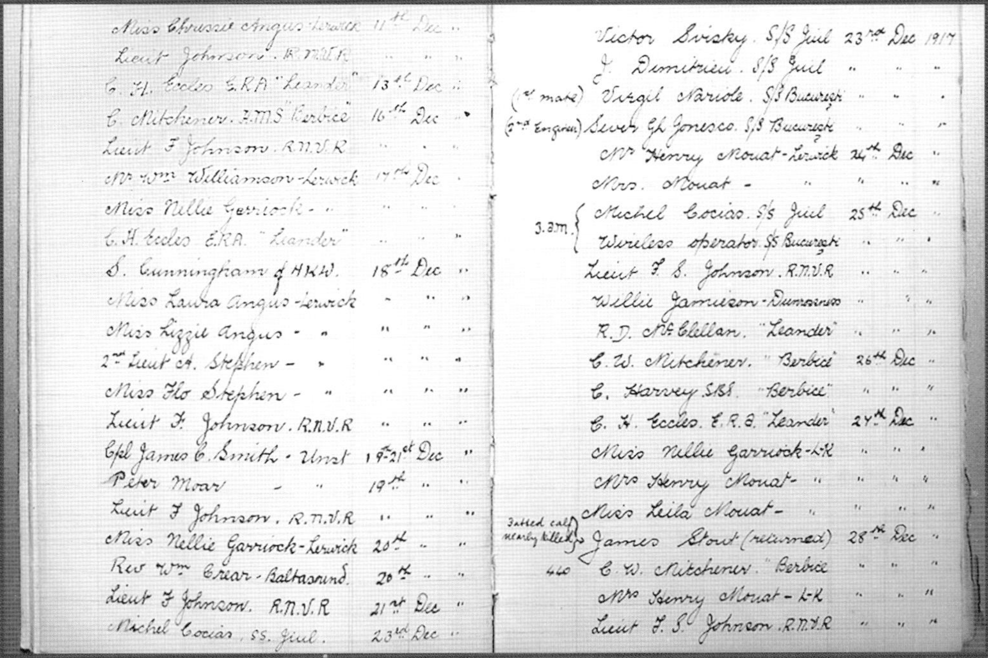

Page 1 (top left)

Miss Chrissie Angus-Lerwick	11th Dec
Lieut. Johnson. R.N.V.R	"
C. H. Eccles E.R.A "Leander"	13th Dec
C. Mitchener. J.M.S "Berbice"	16th Dec
Lieut F. Johnson. R.N.V.R	"
Mr Wm Williamson-Lerwick	17th Dec
Miss Nellie Garriock -	"
C. H. Eccles E.R.A. "Leander"	"
S. Cunningham of H.M.W.	18th Dec
Miss Laura Angus-Lerwick	"
Miss Lizzie Angus - "	"
2nd Lieut A. Stephen - "	"
Miss Flo Stephen - "	"
Lieut F. Johnson. R.N.V.R	"
Cpl James C. Smith - Unst	19-21st Dec
Peter Moar - "	19th "
Lieut F. Johnson. R.N.V.R	"
Miss Nellie Garriock-Lerwick	20th "
Rev Wm Criar - Baltasound	20th "
Lieut F. Johnson. R.N.V.R	21st Dec
Michel Cocias. SS. Juil.	23rd Dec

Page 1 (top right)

Victor Svicky. S/S Juil	23rd Dec 1917
J. Dimitrieu. S/S Juil	"
(1 mate) Virgil Nariole. S/S Bucuresti	"
(3rd Engin) Sever Sp Ionesco. S/S Bucuresti	"
Mr Henry Mouat-Lerwick	24th Dec
Mrs Mouat	"
3.3.M { Michel Cocias. S/S Juil	25th Dec
Wireless operator S/S Bucuresti	"
Lieut F. S. Johnson. R.N.V.R	"
Willie Jamieson-Dunrossness	"
R. D. McClellan. "Leander"	"
C. W. Mitchener. "Berbice"	26th Dec
C. Harvey S.B.S. "Berbice"	"
C. H. Eccles. E.R.A. "Leander"	27th Dec
Miss Nellie Garriock-L.K	"
Mrs Henry Mouat - "	"
Intted calf Miss Leila Mouat -	"
nearly killed } James Stout (returned)	28th Dec
4to C. W. Mitchener. "Berbice"	"
Mrs Henry Mouat - L.K	"
Lieut F. S. Johnson R.N.V.R	"

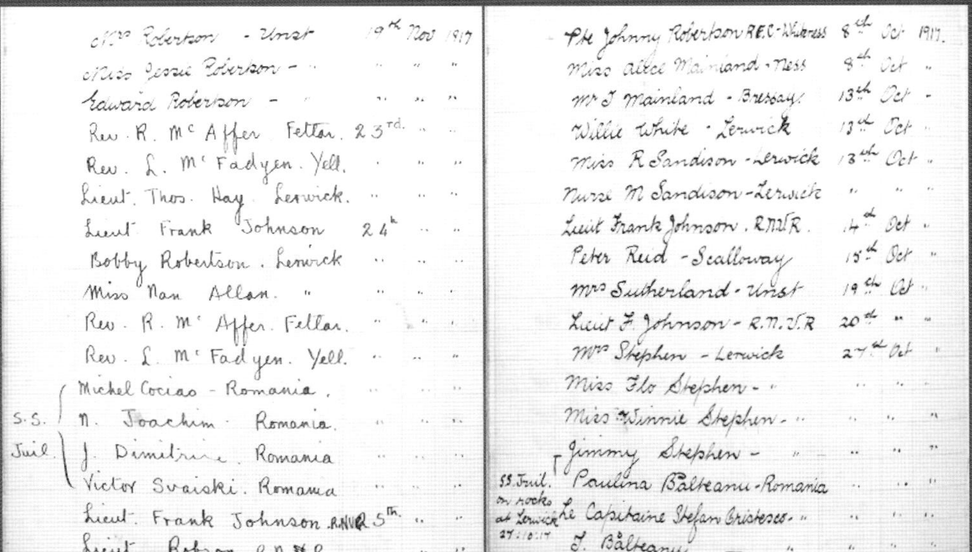

Page 2 (bottom left)

Mrs Robertson - Unst	19th Nov 1917
Miss Jessie Peterson -	"
Edward Robertson -	"
Rev. R. McAffer. Fetlar.	23rd "
Rev. L. McFadyen. Yell.	"
Lieut. Thos. Hay. Lerwick	"
Lieut. Frank Johnson	24th
Bobby Robertson. Lerwick	"
Miss Nan Allan. "	"
Rev. R. McAffer. Fetlar.	"
Rev. L. McFadyen. Yell.	"
Michel Cocias - Romania	"
S.S. { N. Joachim - Romania.	"
Juil { J. Dimitrieu - Romania	"
Victor Svaiski. Romania	"
Lieut. Frank Johnson. R.N.V.R	5th "
Lieut. Robson. R.N.V.R	"
Rev. L. McFadyen	26th "
S.S. { J. Dimitrieu. Romania.	28th
Juil { Victor Svaiski. Romania	"
Joan Sutherland. Lerwick	"

Page 2 (bottom right)

Pte Johnny Robertson R.E.C. Wharves	8th Oct 1917
Miss Alice Mainland - Ness	8th Oct "
Mrs J. Mainland - Bressay	13th Oct -
Willie White - Lerwick	13th Oct "
Miss R Sandison - Lerwick	13th Oct "
Nurse M Sandison - Lerwick	"
Lieut Frank Johnson. R.N.V.R	14th Oct "
Peter Reid - Scalloway	15th Oct
Mrs Sutherland - Unst	19th Oct
Lieut F. Johnson - R.N.V.R	20th "
Mrs Stephen - Lerwick	27th Oct
Miss Flo Stephen -	"
Miss Minnie Stephen -	"
Jimmy Stephen -	"
SS. Juil. Paulina Balteanu - Romania	"
on rocks Capitaine Stefan Cristescu.	"
at Lerwick 27.10.17 J. Balteanu -	"
Elizabetha Balteanu -	"
Struck J. Dimitrieu (mate) -	"
Lieut Frank Johnson R.N.V.R	"
Lieut L P Robson. R.N.R.	"
"Pirate"	

De Hoop passing Bressay Lighthouse.

The Dutch Hospital ship *De Hoop* lying at the pier below the Medical Hall.

Family visit to Sound, Westhall in the background. Mr Stout seated left looking resolutely away from the camera. Daughter Margaret standing left, and seated in front Anne, David Irvine and Dan Harper.

A group of officers in relaxed mood, all were frequent visitors to the Medical Hall.

A party in the Medical Hall, Mr Stout seated on the left.

Mr Stout enjoying the company of the young members of his family and their friends on the beach at Sand.

The drifter *Ruby Gem* was converted to a gun boat in 1918.
Members of the crew were regular visitors to the Medical Hall.

Portrait of Mrs Stout on her wedding day in Edinburgh,
6th October, 1886.

Margaret Mainland Stout 1859-1946

The Years Before the War

1914, and Margaret Mainland Stout had been married to the pharmacist Charles Brown Stout for twenty-eight years and made the Medical Hall her home. She must have been thankful for the time spent at the Edinburgh School of Cookery where she received instruction in housekeeping for a large house and family.

Groceries were purchased from Kay's grocery store across the narrow street from the Medical Hall, and the grocery account was settled once a year! Flour was bought in large quantities and stored in a tin barrel. Melrose's Tea came in a big square tin with an oriental design.

Sugar was bought from a large "sugar cone" which stood on the grocery shop counter, the assistant breaking off the required amount with sturdy sugar tongs.

The Medical Hall property extended to a walled garden a short way up Quendale Lane across the street from the house. Baskets of washing were carried up to the "drying green", and delicious jams and puddings were made from the abundant crop of rhubarb.

Mrs Stout could not have managed the large house and family and the constant stream of visitors without the help of housemaids and nursery maids, which she treated with great kindness and respect.

The young children played in the nursery with the rocking horse Dobbin, the doll's house and other delights, but there was no garden to exercise young limbs on fine days and holidays. Mrs Stout solved this problem by sending children, usually in twos, to relatives in the country, and a nursery maid – who had married a lighthouse keeper – regularly took two little girls to stay with her at the Muckle Flugga Shore Station in Unst.

They loved the freedom of the Burrafirth silver sand beach and enjoyed the attention lavished on two little girls.

Margaret writes of being sent as a small girl on the sailing ship *Columbine* from Lerwick to Dunrossness to stay with her grandparents. The same ship on which

Betty Mouat[1] made her lone voyage to Norway some years later. Margaret was placed in the cabin below decks and the captain put his jacket around her. She said the smell of tobacco made her feel worse than the motion of the ship. Mr Stout had purchased a small property, "Bankfield" outside Lerwick, for two maiden sisters and for the family to use with discretion. They could walk to Bankfield and picnic. The girls loved the buttercup and daisy meadow in contrast to the rocky shore and two straight-laced maiden aunts.

Before 1914 private houses "opened" at Up-Helly-A' to welcome guizers to supper and to dance. The front door of the Medical Hall opened onto Commercial Street and led to the large dining room which was perfect for entertaining guizers and friends. Mrs Stout and family organised the dining room for dancing and refreshments, while Mr Stout was out with his "squad" in the procession. One of his elaborate costumes – "Night and Day" – was stored in the costume trunk and used by the family for guizing. One half of the robe was dark blue with moons and stars embroidered in silver and white thread, while the other half was blue with white clouds and suns glinting in yellow and gold. It sounds wonderful.

Her daughter Margaret wrote, "Mama was very hospitable and there were people coming and going constantly. Country ministers, and visiting clergy from south, always found a welcome and often a bed at the Medical Hall." She devoted time to supporting her church and the British Woman's Temperance Association the BWTA.

Margaret continues,

> Although there were eight of us, she was always adding another child who was more or less homeless. One was a lawyer's daughter, Muriel Bain aged 12. Her mother was blind, her father had left them and gone to Glasgow. There were four children. When the mother was admitted to hospital, four ladies in the town offered to take the four children between them. Poor little Muriel, we just accepted her. She was fed, clothed and educated until the mother died and the father sent for the children.
>
> A knock at the door late one winter's night revealed an old woman wrapped in a shawl, she was a member of the same church as Mama. Her son in law had turned her out of his home. Mama took her in and settled her in an armchair in front of the still warm kitchen fire and no doubt made her a cup of tea. She stayed until lodgings were found for her. She rocked the baby, darned stockings and made herself most useful.

---

1 On the 30th January, 1886, the sailing boat *Columbine* en route from Grutness in the south of Shetland to Lerwick, through a bizarre sequence of events, lost her crew and drifted to Norway with the loan passenger Betty Mouat on board.

Mrs Stout was a strong character and usually made the daily decisions affecting the family. She watched over her brood with love and care but raised them to be independent. They travelled the world with a confidence that stems from a secure and loving home.

Mr and Mrs Stout and family 1905. From left. Mrs Stout, Queenie, Francisca, Margaret, Anne, Elizabeth, Harriet, Charles and Mr Stout, sitting at the front, James.

A group gathering sphagnum moss on the Isle of Noss. Left Mrs Stout, her maid from the Medical Hall, Jessie, Maisie, Georgie and Lottie Jamieson from Noss. Harriet Stout dressed in white, and pride of place, Roy.

Margaret Mainland Stout 1859-1946

The War Years

Mrs Stout's daughter Margaret, returning to Lerwick from college in Edinburgh after the outbreak of war declared, "Mama was engrossed in war work. Queen Mary's Needlework Guild, the Dorcas Society and the Red Cross".

Shetland women in town and country turned their hands to sewing and knitting for the war effort. The Shetland branch of Queen Mary's Needlework Guild (QMNG) was formed in September 1914. The presidents were Mrs Bruce of Sumburgh and Lady Nicolson of Fetlar, there was an organiser for each district and local committees. The headquarters of the Lerwick branch were in the County Hall where members gathered to sew and knit. Mrs Stout was a prominent member of the Lerwick branch and spoke of the many strange and poignant garments she made for amputees such as trousers with one leg or two short legs, and shirts with one arm. Mrs Stout's daughters had never been taught to knit, but when they were at home they sewed diligently for QMNG. In the course of the war more than 15,000 garments had been made in Shetland for QMNG.

After the war the Shetland Branch of QMNG received an invitation from Queen Mary to attend a garden party at Buckingham Palace in recognition of their war work. No one was available to go at such short notice. Mrs Stout suggested that her three daughters who were in London, and who had all participated in war work, could represent Shetland at the garden party. The committee immediately agreed. Harriet, Margaret and Anne were thrilled and honoured to represent their native isles, and set about finding something to wear. Margaret gives an account of the garden party later in the book.

Mrs Stout was a prodigious cook in the Mrs Beeton tradition. She made delicious brawn and game pies, and her daughter Margaret drew on her wide knowledge of traditional Shetland cookery when she was writing, *Cookery for Northern Wives*[1] the

---

1 *Cookery for Northern Wives* by Margaret Bannatyne Stout published by T. Manson, Lerwick 1922. Facsimile published by Shetland Amenity Trust in 2013.

first traditional Shetland recipe book. Mrs Stout posted food parcels to James in France. His favourite plumb cake had been lovingly baked and posted, only to be returned when he was reported missing. The girls thought the worst had happened but decided not to tell their parents until they had definite confirmation of James's fate. At last the good news came that James was wounded and in hospital in Woolwich. Joyously the cake was posted to Woolwich.

Mrs Stout gave generously to the war effort. The set of gamalan drums, a gift from her brother Capt. Henry Mainland from the Philippines, went for scrap metal. An identical set can be seen in Osborne House, Queen Victoria's summer house on the Isle of Wight, among gifts from the Empire. The mahogany family cradle was auctioned for the war effort. The auctioneer, Billy MacKay renowned for his wit, knocked the cradle down to a local dignitary, a bachelor, whom everyone knew had a lady friend and a baby on one of the islands!

Mrs Stout welcomed a steady stream of visitors to the Medical Hall during the war years. Some were friends, some were friends of friends, and some were complete strangers. Mr Stout would meet congenial service men in the shop and invite them to the house, and the girls invited naval officers they had met socially at friend's houses in Lerwick and functions in the Town Hall.

Although the house was awash with servicemen and shipwrecked Romanians, Mrs Stout calmly continued to host committee meetings of the BWTA in the house, and the annual Presbytery tea for ten, including five ministers and the Rev. C. Hicks of the Grand Fleet. She continued to dispense hospitality and often a bed, to the endless procession of ministers from Unst, Yell, Fetlar, Eshaness and Burra Isle. Lerwick friends and relations visited regularly, and those from the country made the Medical Hall their headquarters while attending to business and shopping in Lerwick.

Mrs Stout's cousin, Lance Corporal Jack Sinclair from West Australia, arrived in London on leave from the Western Front and soon received an introduction to Margaret Stout, who was engaged in war work in London. She was coming home on leave and Jack decided to travel to Shetland with her and to continue his leave with the family. Mrs Stout was overjoyed to see her handsome cousin Jack again. Emigration to Australia was so final then. Betty was also on leave from France and Charlie captured the reunion on film.[2]

Mr and Mrs Stout were occasionally persuaded to picnic with the young members of the family, and anniversaries were celebrated by family and friends, at home, with parties and dinners. Mr and Mrs Stout clearly enjoyed these occasions.

The war had tossed people around and now that it was over some were coming home, while others left for far horizons. Queenie, Harriet and Charlie remained in

---

2   See Elizabeth Brown Stout photographs

Shetland, James wounded but able to resume his banking career in Dunfermline. Anne was married and living in China, Betty married to an American naval officer had sailed to America taking her sister Margaret with her.

After Mr Stout died in 1928, Harriet, with the family's approval gave up her nursing career to look after Mrs Stout and oversee the running of the Medical Hall. Anne had returned from China with two children and had made her home in King Harald Street. On a fine Sunday afternoon Mrs Stout would set off in her bath chair propelled by the maid, with Harriet in attendance, to take tea with Anne and her grandchildren. The bath chair was eventually lent to Miss Foster on the Isle of Vaila who suffered from multiple sclerosis. Mrs Stout and Mrs Foster had met at QMNG and they arranged for Miss Foster to seek refuge in the ground floor of the Medical Hall when Mrs Foster was in Lerwick on business.

Mrs Stout made two journeys to America to visit family and friends. She continued to preside over the burgeoning family home. She enjoyed the constant stream of visitors, sons and daughters, husbands and wives, and now grandchildren, all who loved her dearly.

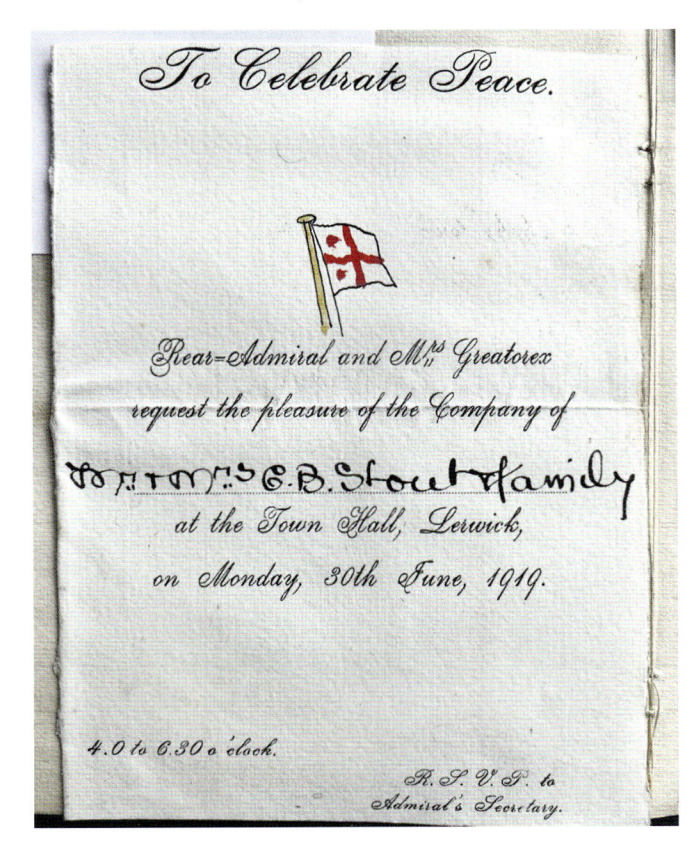

An invitation from Rear Admiral and Mrs Greatorex to Mr and Mrs Stout and family to a peace celebration in the Town Hall, Lerwick, 30th June, 1919.

Mrs Margaret Mainland Stout with daughters
Harriet (left) and Margaret (right).

Mrs Stout presiding over lunch in the Medical Hall.

Willa, a maid in the Medical Hall.

Snooks the house cat.

Mr and Mrs Stout's 40th wedding anniversary. A family supper party and musical evening with Stouts, Mouats, Campbells, Mainlands, and Dr Yule.

Lieut. Frank Johnson RNVR, on board one of the hydrophone boats.

Mr and Mrs Stout enjoying a moment on a family picnic.
They were quietly devoted to each other.

Mrs Stout resplendent in her bath chair.

Anne with her bicycle at the back of the Medical Hall.

Anne Elizabeth Stout 1887-1976

The Years Before the War

Anne Elizabeth Stout was twenty seven years old in 1914 and assistant teacher in Hamnavoe School, Burra Isle, where her sister Betty was headmistress.

Anne was the eldest daughter and set the educational pattern for all the girls. They attended the Anderson Educational Institute in Lerwick and continued their studies at college or university in Edinburgh or Glasgow, and pursued careers at a time when careers for women living in the far-flung Shetland Islands, were in their infancy.

Mrs Stout visited Edinburgh to arrange digs for the girls, while they attended college. Mr Stout gave each an adequate allowance for the term, and they would never have asked for a penny more.

In order to attend Moray House Training College in Edinburgh with Betty, her younger sister, Anne spent a year as a student teacher at St Dunstan's Lady's College in Broadstairs Kent. She studied a wide range of subjects and taught French and German. She and Betty were now in a position to attend college together and share digs.

Anne was very musical. All the girls had received piano lessons from a teacher in Lerwick but Anne also displayed a talent for stringed instruments. She was particularly fond of her ornate Italian mandolin. Anne wrote poetry and prose for publication and contributed to the literary life of the town. Her speeches and lectures were punctuated by extensive use of classical literature and poetry. She was artistic and always beautifully and correctly dressed, you never saw her without hat and gloves, even fishing!

She took her church duties seriously and was secretary to the Shetland branch of the British Women's Temperance Association. She was thoughtful and kind to others and deeply caring for children. Friends and younger sisters sought her advice and loved her dearly.

Anne playing her lute with cousin May on her violin.

Anne and David Webster Irvine sharing a toast at dinner in the Medical Hall.

Anne serving tea in the Medical Hall.

Portrait of Anne in the uniform of the Scottish Church's Huts, Cologne.

Anne Elizabeth Stout 1887-1976

The War Years

Shetland News 1918:

> Ever since the outbreak of hostilities in 1914 Miss Stout has been an indefatigable war worker, and has devoted almost all her spare time to canteen work at Alexandra Wharf, endeavouring to brighten the lot of servicemen based in Lerwick and latterly in entertaining fishermen and others in the Missions to Seamen Hut, with musical evenings. She employed her needlework skills to sewing garments for Queen Mary's Needlework Guild, and her literary skills in executive and propaganda work for the war effort.

From April 1917, Anne, who was teaching at the Central School in Lerwick, spent most of her spare time working in the Scottish Church Army Hut at Alexandra Wharf, where servicemen gathered for refreshments, company and musical evenings. From the photograph the interior does not look very inviting, but the welcome was.

The hut became a focus for fund raising for the war effort and contributed £209 to endow the "Lerwick" bed at Rouyaumont, the Scottish Women's hospital in France, for wounded servicemen. The hut was also used as a distribution centre for food and clothing for men and women rescued from ships torpedoed in Shetland waters. We have already read of Anne's roll in assisting the shipwrecked Romanians from the SS *Juil* to find accommodation in Lerwick and an invitation to the Medical Hall where they received hospitality. Anne and Captain Stefan Christesco conversed in French; he had written books in French on relativity in opposition to Einstein. He gave two signed copies to Anne.

Anne, like her sisters, was not stage-shy, and took part in dramatic productions, in aid of war funds. She had a leading role in a highly successful entertainment held in the Town Hall for King George's Fund for Sailors, as Lady Penzance, in a production of "Poached Eggs and Pearls!" She continued her stage career in a skit "A War Committee" which made good natured fun of those ladies anxious "to do something" and who accomplished little more than good intentions. This went down very well with the audience who recognised certain local ladies characterised in the cast.

The army needed men. Millions of men. Throughout Britain women were encouraged to persuade young men to join the army and shame those who were "shirkers".

James George Peterson was the message boy in D.&G. Kay's grocery shop across the street from the Medical Hall where the Stouts bought all their groceries. James must have confided in Anne that he wanted to enlist and, Anne keen to "do her bit", paved the way for James to join the Gordon Highlanders. To mark the occasion she invited James to tea in the Medical Hall where he became affectionately known as "Annie's recruit". Poor Anne was mortified, on reflection, when she realised what the consequences could be, and spent the remaining war years anxiously scanning the lists of dead and wounded in the reading room.

To everyone's relief James George Peterson survived the war despite being seriously gassed in France in September 1918. He never knew the anxiety he had caused one young lady.

During the war years friends asked Anne to write obituaries for their relatives who were casualties of the war. She was deeply saddened when she found herself writing obituaries for former members of her navigation class.

Anne enjoyed writing in verse, and her poem "The Bugle Band", inspired after hearing them in the street, was published in *The Shetland News*. The pithy reply from the "domestic" was printed the following week. Anne was mortified that her sentiments had been misconstrued.

The Shetland Times 14th March, 1916.

THE BUGLE BAND

There's a sudden distant rumble
And a mighty tootle – too,
There's a banging and a clanging
And a fearful how-d'you-do,
There's a rushing and a hushing
Of the folk who stand about,
And a lifting up of windows
When the R.N.R. turns out.

All the traffic is suspended.
While the Lads in Blue march by,
Soup for dinner left unattended
Starts to burn on the sly,
While the erring young domestic,

Heedless of the smell of soot,
Sees her brother wield the drumsticks
While another blows a flute.

Sometimes 'tis the wail of bagpipes
Sometimes 'tis a ragtime gay,
Off to church or off to battle
Music cheers them on the way.
Though the powers that be above us
Money or our life demand,
We will never be downhearted,
While we have the bugle band.

A.E.S. Lerwick, March 1916.

Anne received a complimentary note on her poem from Lieut. Col. Philips RMLI OC Shetland Section RNR.

The Shetland Times 18th March, 1916. The reply from the Domestic.

THE BUGLE BAND
To A.E.S.

Am glad to see that A.E.S.
Has tried her hand at rhyme,
I often thought to do the same
But never could get time.

The world has changed so much of late
And husbands getting few,
I'll let the hurry all go by
And write a line or two.

I am an honest working lass
The pay I get is small,
I wash and scrub and cook the meals
And answer every call.

But when I see the children run
I know my love is coming,
I let the stew go up the lum
And watch the drummers drumming.

> What care I for soup or stew
> Or Madam heard to please,
> I hear the wail of a new war song
> A wafted on the breeze.
>
> A.E.S. may never feel
> The joy that I conceal,
> While she goes scalding up and down
> All o'er a ruined meal.
>
> C.A.M. (The Domestic)

Although the war ended in November 1918 there was still work for the Scottish Church's Huts, now with the Army of Occupation in Germany.

Anne takes up the story:

> The Scottish Church's Huts had made an urgent appeal for voluntary workers for their club in Cologne, the headquarters of the British Army of the Rhine. I sent in an application and was accepted. I had the necessary qualifications – knowledge of German, cookery, first aid and canteen experience and it was a heaven sent opportunity to see for myself the aftermath of the war which had engulfed our lives for the last four years. I resigned from my teaching post at the Central School in Lerwick and set off for London, where I stayed with my sisters Margaret and Harriet. I was there when the invitations arrived for the three of us to attend the Garden Party at Buckingham Palace for members of Queen Mary's Needlework Guild.

Anne wore the becoming uniform of the Scottish Church's Soldier's Clubs to the garden party and looks stunning in the studio photograph of the three sisters taken on that memorable day. Margaret wrote an account of the garden party.

Anne left London for Germany the next day 26th July, 1919, to take up her duties with the Scottish Church's Soldier's Club in Cologne. She travelled by train from Boulogne to Cologne over some of the most fought over ground of the war. Calais, St Omer, Hazlebrouck, Valenciennes, Mons, (where the last shot of the war was fired) Charleroi, Namur, Liege, Frontier, Duren and finally Cologne.

From the train Anne had her first sight of the war-torn landscape pitted with shell holes and abandoned trenches already partially covered with soft green grass and creeping plants. She saw many towns and villages reduced to heaps of rubble, with only a splintered church spire piercing the sky.

The retreating German army had destroyed all the bridges and the train progressed slowly over temporary crossings replaced by the Royal Engineers. They passed German freight trains taking captured German and British guns bound for England. They waved to passing troop trains filled with British soldiers singing and waving on their way home.

Cologne was the capitol of Rhineland, the British Occupation Zone, and the headquarters of the British Army of the Rhine. Anne continues her diary with her arrival at the Scottish Church's Club in Cologne.

> Our canteen was a commandeered hotel and proudly flies the Scottish flag over the main entrance in the heart of the capital of Rhineland, where it can be seen by the busy teeming multitudes every day. The soldiers walk about as if Cologne and Rhineland belonged to them! And so it should be. The building is not beautiful but how loving is the warm welcome from six ladies who toil from morning to night, seven days a week, and earn the undying gratitude of countless weary homesick men.
>
> On the ground floor there is a big restaurant with little round tables and numerous chairs generally crowded with men. Near the door is a well-stocked canteen where Jack or Tommy can buy all the small necessities of army life from cigarettes to bootlaces. At the back is the worker's dining room, and upstairs reading and writing rooms, a library and a quiet room where soldiers can study and talk with the Chaplin. There is also a hall where popular services are held on Sunday evenings.
>
> The top flat consists of bedrooms which we occupy, though some of the staff slept out with German families.

Anne's fluency in German was proving very useful and she found her services were constantly in demand. She translated the appeal by Burgomaster Kalpers which had appeared on posters all over Cologne reminding the German people to be courteous towards the British Army of Occupation. "Citizens are earnestly requested to maintain great calm and order on the entry of the Entente Troops into our city and to receive them with courtesy and dignity."

Ann describes the Sunday evening services as being well attended.

> The men sang the old hymns till the street echoed and crowds of wandering Germans gathered below the windows. There is one hymn which is set to the tune of their national anthem "Deutschland Uber Alles" and the singing of this never failed to draw a crowd.
>
> Officially we were attached to the Lowland Division with clubs in eight other

towns but Cologne, as the centre for demobilisation, saw soldiers of every regiment passing through, and all were made equally welcome. When I tell you that we drew on average £180 a day, and on occasion, £230 you will realise that life at the Sign of the Thistle was no picnic!

However, there was a certain amount of off duty time, and I took full advantage of this to see as many places as possible. Being in uniform we had the privilege of free travel on all buses, trains and boats in the occupied area, an opportunity not to be missed.

The Rhine is the most beautiful river in Europe and every inch of its banks is crowded with history, romance and legend, and now I had the opportunity to visit the places I had read about in classical German literature. The rock where the Loreli sang to lure sailors to their death, the island where Siegfred slew the dragon and so on. In company with other workers I travelled here and there crossing and recrossing this wonderful river and sailing as far as Mainz, the headquarters of the American and French forces respectively.

I visited Bruhl, Godesberg, Trier, Zons and of course explored Cologne. As the name implies it is of Roman origin, and the city is built in rings like a huge spider's web. Its glory is it's lovely twin towered cathedral which took five centuries to build, the stone for which was quarried from the famous Dragon's Rock, one of the seven mountains of Bonn. The origin of the name refers to the slaying of a dragon there by "Siegfried".

Anne recalls an amusing experience at Bonn which occurred while they were looking for the world-famous university to see original manuscripts of Beethoven's music.

A small boy of about 10 years, sitting on a step reading a book, addressed us in French and asked if we were looking for anyplace in particular. We replied in the same language and he offered to be our guide. We chatted for some time, then I noticed he wore a replica of an iron cross in his buttonhole. "How is it," I said, "that you a French boy are wearing an iron cross?" "But I am German," he retorted, "I speak French because you are French." "Indeed we are not," I replied, "we are Scottish." "Ah" his eyes lit up, "I know Scots – My hearts in the highlands my heart is not here – My hearts in the highlands a-chasing the deer". We burst out laughing and he looked very offended. "You laugh at my bad English – ja?" We hastened to assure him that we only laughed at the quotation and I asked him if he could speak any other languages besides French and English. "Oh yes – Latin I know and I study Spanish of myself." "Why Spanish?" I said. "Well you see – Germany must try to get new markets after this war, and South America will be one, so I learn Spanish to be ready."

Anne Elizabeth Stout 1887-1976

I have since wondered if the name of this wonder-child was Ribbenthrop! (Joachin Von Ribbenthorp became Foreign Minister for Nazi Germany.)

Anne and her companions soon found themselves swept into a social whirl which had accelerated as soon as the war ended.

I was escorted to balls in the Kaiser's Palace in Bonn which claimed to have the most magnificent staircase in Europe. The lower part of the Kaiser's palace had been taken over by the W.M.C.A. and the "doings" there would have made Kaiser Bill's hair stand on end. Zons was a small walled town on the banks of the Rhine and the headquarters of the King's Own Scottish Borderers, and I shall not readily forget a regimental dinner there at which we danced eightsome reels to the bagpipes while a gaping crowd looked in the open windows at what must have seemed to them the maddest antics yet of the Mad British.

These were lean days for the Germans. I remember asking for a cup of tea in a hotel and getting the most dreadful "substitute" I have ever tasted – it was like a decoction of stale hay! Two workers and myself visited the house where they had been billeted for a time. The hausfrau greeted them like long lost prodigals. She insisted on a meal and having nothing else made "Reiber Kuchen" – that is raw potato grated down made into cakes and fried. They tasted very nice and she gave us some in a paper to eat in the train on the way home! She told us how all her brass taps, handles and cooking pots had been taken by the soldiers to make munitions.

Anne describes a visit to a fort near Lindenthal built after the Franco Prussian War and now the headquarters of an anti-aircraft battery.

It was a grim sort of a place, with a mote, a drawbridge, underground cells and oubliettes. These last were diabolical traps: you stood unsuspectingly on one and it gave way beneath your feet tipping you down into a sort of well with sharp spikes imbedded in cement pointing upwards. The top of the fort was camouflaged with grass and trees to be invisible from the air. Brocklemund was the name and I hope our men blew it up before they left the Rhine.

Winston Churchill paid a visit to Cologne while Anne was there:

In the vicinity was a wood with a clearing where a grand military tattoo was held in honour of the visit of Winston Churchill on the 18th of August. It was a wonderful spectacle, the dark night showing up the torches and fireworks to full advantage while the massed bands of twelve battalions rendered stirring marches, finishing up with "Abide with me". The following day Winston reviewed the troops and we had the honour of being included.

Anne must have seen Churchill at very close quarters – but she makes no comment. This story, told by Anne in her war diaries, tells of a strange coincidence which took place in their canteen.

A nice Scottish boy was a regular visitor both to meals and services. He always sat at the same little table had a cup of tea and a bun and read his morning newspaper. One morning when I was on duty and had served him, one of the workers came bustling in with a sprig of heather. "I got this from my sister" she said, "and she wants me to give it to a Scottish soldier" "Well", I said, "there's a nice young lad sitting there, shall I give it to him?" "Why yes," she said, "and here is the little card that goes with it". On the card was the senders name and the place where the heather was gathered. I took it over to the table where the boy sat and without a word laid it on his plate. He looked as if he had seen a ghost! Then he came to the counter and holding the heather lovingly in his hand said, "Do you know that this heather is picked from near my home and the lady was my Sunday school teacher". Now wasn't that a strange coincidence, out of all the hundreds who came to our club to fix on that one boy who had been her Sunday school pupil! We christened him the "Heather Boy", and four years later, when I was in Glasgow getting my outfit for China, he and his fiancée came and saw us off at the station.

Another surprise was a visit from Captain Peter Hutchison in the uniform of an army chaplain. When I had last seen him he was in the RNR and a member of my evening continuation class in Navigation in Shetland!

The only other Shetlander I met was Bobby Gilbertson whom I trailed to the top of Cologne Cathedral – a fearsome climb"

On 4th October they had their farewell service for the men, and on the 9th the canteen was officially closed, "and we packed up and went our various ways. Another worker and myself made a leisurely tour of the battlefields and front line, but that is another story".

The battlefields held a fascination for people trying to understand what the major theatre of operations was really like. The Armistice was followed by requests from civilians to visit the battlefields, some out of curiosity, some searching for their dead.

On 18th November Winston Churchill, Secretary of State for War, made the following announcement. "At present and for some months to come, it would be impossible, owing to military reasons, for civilians to visit the Battle Fields."

The Battle zones were a wasteland, utterly impassable in many places, hazardous unexploded shells, ammunition and the bodies of the dead, littered the ground. The infrastructure was primitive and much under military control. To gain access to Ypres civilians needed a special pass. Anne and her colleague were travelling on their own, but in uniform, which permitted them to travel on railways, explore the battlefields and ruined towns, and seek accommodation. Official arrangements were made for groups of nurses who had been working in France and Belgium, to visit the battlefields and see the conditions under which their patients had lived and fought. The former inhabitants of these wastelands were beginning to trickle back to search among the rubble for whatever remained of their homes, and those that stayed created small pockets of life.

From 1920 the number of visitors grew to a flood. The former inhabitants, living in hastily erected huts, soon realised that visitors needed refreshments, souvenirs and guides, and the income generated became a major part of the local economy. Several travel companies operated battlefield tours. The Franco British Travel Bureau offered "Battlefield Tours de Lux" manned by ex-officers and with deluxe cars. It was recommended that visitors wore "thick soled stout boots, took a walking stick, sandwiches and something to drink". It is hard to equate "tourism" with the reality of blood-soaked battlefields where thousands had so recently died.

Anne continues her diary with telling accounts of their travels on the Western Front in October and November 1919, eleven months after the Armistice.

> To go back the way we came did not sound very interesting so another worker and myself decided to see something of the battlefields which had dominated our thoughts, for four years. The Daily Mail were already producing maps of the Western Front, so I sent for two maps of areas we hoped to explore.
>
> Leaving Cologne at 11.30pm the evening of 15th October we found ourselves in Brussels at 8 next morning, with all our luggage and not the faintest idea of where we would stay. The obvious thing was to hire a conveyance and begin a tour of the hotels. By good luck we struck one which had the arresting sign "Anglo Belge Y.M.C.A." here, for six francs a night bed and breakfast could be procured, with meals a la carte. That it was popular was evident by the number of English officers, nurses and others in residence. Then and there we engaged rooms and felt that fortune was smiling on our expedition.
>
> That afternoon was spent in an orgy of sightseeing. Unfortunately the street cars were all on strike, and as taxis were unprocurable, we had to do our best on shank's mare, and spent a lot of time going from one place to another. The Royal Palace, the Palais de Justice where Nurse Edith Cavell's trial took place, the Cathedral with it's wonderful pulpit carved out of a single piece of oak representing the Temptation,

and finally the Lace Shops which we could hardly pass, so fascinating the dainty merchandise therein, sum up my impression of Brussels. At night the town was illuminated and great rejoicings took place it being the anniversary of the town's deliverance from the Germans.

The following day was occupied by an expedition to Louvain where rubble heaps represent all that is left of the famous library and where marks of sacrilege and wanton destruction meet one at every road.

On 28th August, 1914, German troops in Louvain, in response to "illegal civilian resistance" pursued a reign of terror by burning, looting and executing hundreds of civilians as an example to what happens to those who resist mighty Germany. For five days the city burnt. One fifth of the city was destroyed. The burning of the 13th century university and priceless library of rare books and manuscripts and was seen as an attack on the cultural heritage of all Europe. Germany had descended from being a nation of high culture to one of barbarism akin to Attila the Hun. The name "Hun" stuck. The German strategy of terror did not evoke fear but anger amongst all civilised people. A popular recruiting march in Britain was "Louvain Shall be our Battle Cry!"

Anne writes:

Returning to Brussels we visited the Duke of Wellington's House and saw the room, quite a small one with parquet floor, where the ball took place on the eve of Waterloo. In the evening we went to the opera and saw "Carmen". It seemed so strange to hear so much French spoken after getting used to German.

The following morning they left by train for Lille in northern France. The journey took them by Mons, Le Chateau. Cambrai, Arras, Vimy, Lens and finally Lille. Anne saw from the train window the battle-scarred landscape around Arras where her brother James, with the Seaforth Highlanders, had been wounded in a senseless battle in 1917.

On arriving in Lille their first thought was to find somewhere to stay.

This town was such a convenient centre for seeing the battlefields that it was crowded with visitors and after driving from one hotel to another, it was with great satisfaction that a haven of refuge was found in the Hotel Belleville, a gorgeous place, comfortable and luxurious. Some parts of Lille had been destroyed but only a few ruins came under our notice during our short stay.

In October 1914 Lille had endured a ten-day siege, and the population had been made to suffer under German occupation. Hostages were taken to secure obedience and allied prisoners were paraded daily to undermine the morale of French citizens. The German military requisitioned cafes and restaurants where German soldiers could relax on leave from the front.

The following morning Anne and her companion took an early train to Armentiers. The train travelled slowly over some of the most fought over ground in France.

> The landscape approaching Armentiers, was a sea of mud and shell holes filled with rainwater, remains of trenches, gun emplacements, and barbed wire entanglements. The poor trees were all standing split and dead, and over towards the town is one sad chaotic scene of bricks and mortar, stone walls and skeletons of houses. No one lives here anymore.

Towards the end of the war Armentiers was assaulted with mustard gas and abandoned. The town and surrounding area had been designated part of Zone Rouge, an area of total destruction.

> The journey from Lille to Armentiers took about three quarters of an hour. It was like a city of the dead. Not a soul to be seen except a solitary Tommy hurrying back to his base somewhere amongst the desolation of the surrounding battlefields. The town had been totally destroyed by shell fire, houses which were not lying in heaps seemed ready to topple at any moment. It was a strange feeling to be peering at the remains of other people's lives. I picked up a pottery tile, unbroken, from a pile of debris. We wandered for hours among ruins going as far as Le Bisset a village which had been entirely destroyed. Here, to our amazement, in a tiny dugout of a house we found a cheerful little Belgium woman getting her small family ready for Church! A button was being sewed to the coat of a little girl, who with prayer book in hand, was impatient to be off. Where were they going? As the children walked hand in hand down the remains of the sunlight road amidst the ruins, we talked with the mother and found that she and her family had fled to England as refugees and retained the happiest impressions of their stay there. Now they had come back to the ruins of their former home and were bravely facing the future. She had a few postcards for sale and some little odds and ends and looked forward to the influx of visitors expected in the spring.
>
> We returned to Armentiers and paid a visit to the English Cemetery where between four and five thousand British soldiers are buried. Little crosses marked each sacred spot and most had flowers and everything beautifully kept. In a separate part were 900 German graves, but they had no flowers.
>
> A further half hour's journey took us to the ruins of Baillenil. The town had been a rear-guard base for the British army until taken by the Germans in 1914 and

held until August 1918. The British shelled the town almost every day. 98% of the town was destroyed including the ancient Bell Tower. Walking out of the town with the debris of war all around us, we were shown the well-built German front line trenches, separated by only the width of a road in some places, from our trenches. We climbed down a wooden ladder into the trench, and entered into a passage with spaces for two tiers of stretchers for the wounded, beyond were a series of small rooms, one still had a notice pinned up showing precautions to take in the event of a gas attack. We were impressed with the sets of gas tight doors, but glad to climb back out into the sunlight. Our guide pointed out Mount Kemmel in the distance, the scene of one of the most ferocious battles of the war. Thousands of French soldiers died defending this area of strategic importance which the Germans occupied, and held, until it was recaptured by the French in September 1918.

The glorious sunshine gave this desolate wilderness, a beauty of its own. We returned to Armentiers and paid a visit to the Y.M.C.A. hut at the station for much needed refreshment. We spoke with a soldier there, and when I mentioned that we were hoping to find empty shell cases to keep as souvenirs, but were terrified of picking up an unexploded one, he took us to a salvage dump nearby and found for me two brass shell cases which I will take home.

On a lighter note a favourite wartime song, was of course, "Madamoiselle From Armentiers Parlez-vous".

The following morning we made an early departure once more for Belgium. This time our destination was Poperinghe nine miles from Ypres which we reached about 11am and were fortunate once more in finding rooms at the well-known Skindles Hotel. This place, run by Belgians, was a home from home to war weary officers during the fierce fighting around Ypres and is now the most popular rendezvous for visitors to the Belgian battlefields.

Poperinghe, known to the troops as "Pops", was the forward base for the Ypres Salient, the rail centre for supplies to the front line and a casualty clearing station. It was also known to the troops for recreation and rest from duty in the front line. Thousands of troops passed through Pops and were billeted in the area. The town is also famous for Talbot House, a haven of rest for servicemen.

In December 1915 two Army Chaplains, the Rev. P.S.B."Tubby" Clayton and the Rev. Neville Talbot opened Talbot House as a refuge for servicemen in memory of Lt. Gilbert Talbot, a brother, who had been killed at Hooge in July 1915. It was an "Everymans Club" and a notice reminding soldiers that rank held no sway, greeted arrivals: "All Rank Abandon, All Ye Who Enter Here". The club was a huge success. 76 servicemen were accommodated one night! This was the start of what became known as the Toc H movement. Toc H was the army signalling phonetic for T.H. – Talbot House.

The Town Hall in the Main Square held grim associations. It was the Divisional Headquarters during the war, and below the courtyard were the execution cells where soldiers awaited their fate. To see the graffiti, "Canada" on one of the cell walls brings home the harsh realities of war and thoughts of Kipling's poem, "Blindfold and alone". Anne does not mention this sad place in her diary. Poperinghe was targeted by German long-range guns but this does not seem to have deterred those soldiers seeking refuge away from the frontline.

" We took the train to Ypres, the holy ground of British arms, where a quarter of a million British soldiers laid down lives during that immortal stand which will go down to history as the greatest feat of human endurance." On the October, 1914, eight thousand soldiers of the Imperial German Army arrived in Ypres, ordered 8,000 loaves of bread to be baked for delivery at 8am the next morning, raided the town's coffers, and left a bewildered populace at noon. A few days later British and French soldiers arrived in Ypres to take up defensive positions to block the route of the German army to the coastal ports.

The Allies occupied a large semi-circular bulge of low-lying land to the south of the city which bordered the German front line and became known as the Ypres Salient. The low-lying waterlogged clay-based soil of the Salient flooded when the natural drainage channels were destroyed by shelling. The German army had secured superior positions on higher ground around the edge of the Salient. The Allies, however, were determined to defend Ypres at all costs, and for the next four years, thousands of allied soldiers, living in deplorable conditions, died in ferocious battles.

> As we stepped off the train wishing to make the most of our time we appealed to three soldiers who had also got off the train for directions. They looked at us with dull dazed expressions and had the appearance of men who had wakened out of a terrible dream, the horror of which still clung to them. Our sympathetic queries soon drew from them a pitiful story. That very morning in company with their comrades they had lit a fire in a clearing and squatting round were preparing for breakfast when the heat of the fire caused an underground mine or shell to explode with terrific force and of a group of ten or so, these were the sole survivors. They had been in hospital since with shell shock and were now on their way back to camp, but it was evident that they were still suffering from their dreadful experience. We persuaded them into a Y.W.C.A. hut nearby and after warm cups of tea and something to eat and smoke we had the satisfaction of seeing some of the hopelessness die out of their faces.

This was our introduction to Ypres and brought forcibly to our notice the dangerous nature of the work on which so many of our soldiers are now engaged, that of clearing up the debris of battle. Carrying on amid dreary and depressing surroundings with none of the excitement of battle to sustain, and never knowing at what moment something unforeseen might leap up as it were from the ground to maim or kill, our labour battalions need all the sympathy and help that can be given them. Many a gruesome find they have, and much melancholy work has to be done before the scattered graves of nameless heroes can be gathered together in one last quiet resting place. Participation in this work is voluntary, but a young officer at the camp said "it is the least we can do for the boys".

As the war edged backwards and forwards Ypres and the surrounding countryside became the muddiest, bloodiest scene of conflict at terrible cost to human life. The Germans introduced their new weapon, poison gas. At the beginning of May 1915 all the remaining inhabitants were evacuated leaving the ruined city to the troops and the war.

Anne and her companion continued to explore the ruins that were Ypres.

We found another guide in a young soldier who seemed at a loose end and glad of something to break the monotony and offered to take us around. The remains of the ruined spire of St Martin's Cathedral marked the centre of town and he told us something of life in Ypres during the war, as we walked towards the Cathedral. During daylight hours the ruined town was deserted, the soldiers hidden in cellars or among the wreckage of buildings, no one wanted to be seen as a target for the German guns, but at night the town came alive with working parties maintaining trenches and communications, moving troops and supplies of arms and food forward to the lines.

The enormous stone ruins of the once magnificent Cathedral were a sobering sight and one which I shall long and sadly remember. Our guide told us the harrowing story of the forty allied soldiers who had sought shelter in the Cathedral vaults only to be buried alive when shells shattered the interior. Eighteen were dug out alive but twenty-two were dead.

We were conducted to the ruins of the vast Medieval Cloth Hall, one of the jewels of Europe, ravaged by shells and burnt until nothing remained. And then on to the famous Canadian Ramparts which made history. These ramparts have been bought by the Canadian Government and are to be kept intact as a memorial to the fallen. The trenches were just as the men left them, duck boards and all. We entered a dugout in splendid preservation, with the name "Osborne House" and the date 1917 cut in the concrete, inspected pill boxes and scrambled over barbed wire.

Anne Elizabeth Stout 1887-1976

We walked someway along the Menin Road, the scene of so much pain and suffering. The road, the main supply route for food and ammunition to the front line, was shelled day and night by the enemy, and vehicles and men had to make bold dashes under cover of darkness.

For miles we saw only devastation. Every yard of ground had been torn up, a terrible place of mud and shell holes. Abandoned remains of tanks and vehicles were slowly sinking into the morass, shell holes filled with liquid mud became death traps. Blackened tree stumps relieved this desolate landscape and here and there a small sea of crosses.

On the way back a church was passed where everything was in ruins except the figure of Christ on the Cross – a solemn and impressive spectacle. When darkness fell we went back to the Y.W.C.A. and talked to the men assembled there until train time.

The following day our objective was Poelcapelle beyond Ypres and in the direction of Roulers which we reached at noon. Of this village of 7000 inhabitants not a person nor a building remained and the rent and torn ground was strewn with the battered remains of tanks which had come to an untimely end. One still had the remains of two soldiers in its tangled twisted interior, it being impossible to get at the bodies without blowing the whole thing up. We thought we were alone in this desolate landscape and were amazed to hear that the news of our arrival in this region had spread and a friendly disposed officer hurried after us with an invitation to lunch! In the mess room which was a little wooden shack lined with pack sheet and ornamented with stencilled designs by the artistic inhabitants, displaying the crests of Oxford Universities. After a welcome repast our Officer conveyed us some way along the road to Passchendaal pointing out places where battles had been fought. "I lost many good friends here".

We saw no one in this vast wasteland which so recently had been the battlefield for thousands. Only a lonely cross here and there or a small group of crosses bore testament to the soldiers who died here. And we thought of the thousands who had no grave. This wasn't trench warfare any more but a wild dash from shell hole to shell hole never knowing if you would drown in the liquid mud. We could not but think of the wounded struggling in this morass.

The detritus of war was all around us choking in the mud, shell cases, barbed wire, helmets and shreds of clothing blue, grey and khaki all tangled together. We both felt numbed by the enormity of war. Our Officer took us back to the ruins of the station to catch the train to Poperinghe and we thanked him for his hospitality "It was a pleasure –we don't see many English ladies here".

The next morning we reluctantly left this most interesting region and entrained for Bruges changing at Roulers and finally arriving at our destination about 3.20 in the afternoon. We found a delightful hotel in the Market Square just opposite the famous Belfry and spent the evening seeing the sights of the town.

A quainter more romantic place it would be difficult to imagine. The canals wind through the city giving it a Venice-like appearance and making it a paradise for artists and the lovers of the picturesque.

Next morning saw us making an early start for Dixmunde which we reached about 11am. The town was a heap of ruins with here and there a little estaminet or souvenir booth making a brave show amongst the debris.

Page 31 and 32 of the diary are sadly missing but we know what they would have seen at Dixmunde but who they met and what they thought we will never know.

By the time the war ended in 1918 Dixmunde had been reduced to rubble. Dixmunde was the gateway to the Channel ports of Calais and Boulogne and had to be defended at all costs. In October 1914 the floodgates holding back the River Yser were opened flooding the vast plain and holding back the German advance. The river Yser became the front line. In 1915 under heavy fire the Belgians started to dig a complex trench system on the West bank of the Yser with galleries, firesteps, concrete duck boards and sandbags. After three years of incessant attacks, through the use of saps[1], both sides had got closer and closer until only yards apart! In 1917 the Belgian army built a large concrete shelter with lookout holes called the Mouse Trap to stop the Germans infiltrating the Belgium trenches at the end of the saps. Thousands of Belgium and French soldiers lost their lives in what became known as the Trenches of Death and which remained at the heart of Belgian resistance throughout the war. Anne and her companion would have been shown the Trenches of Death, the Mouse Trap and the proximity of the front-line German trenches.

Their next port of call was Zeebruge where they witnessed the aftermath of the British raid on the port to destroy the anchorage for U-boats. The plan was to sink ancient cruisers filled with concrete to block the passage of the U-boats to the sea. Unfortunately it was not a success. The eight VCs awarded drew attention away from the huge loss of life.

Anne writes of their day spent in Zeebruge:

> Next day was spent in Zeebruge where there is much of interest to see. Walking along the Mole one came on Capt. Fryate's ship the "Brussels" which has been refloated and is now being made ready for sea again. One of the men engaged in this work was a Shetlander, but as he had gone on leave the day before, he missed

---

[1] "Sap" a trench dug out from the frontline trench into no-mans-land for closer observance of the enemy.

seeing a fellow countryman. The "Thetis" and the "Iphegenia" are still partially submerged but are being gradually refloated and beached on the sands. Nearby we saw the graves of the heroes of the "Invicta" among whom are those awarded the Victoria Cross. We lunched on the sands enjoying the glorious sea air and autumn sunshine before returning to Bruges. That night I fell asleep to the strains of Haydn's symphony played by the carillon across the square. The following day we said farewell and entrained for Ostend and home.

On her return to Shetland Anne gave a series of lectures on her work with the Scottish Churches Canteen in Cologne, and her visit to the Western Front.

The Shetland News 1918:

Miss Stout gave stirring and vivid impressions of her visit to the Battlefields, and made one feel no written account could describe the desolation wrought by the war in that fair and fertile country. She illustrated her talk with maps, plans and photographs. Interestingly, she concluded her lecture by showing her audience some of the remarkable substitutes the Germans had invented during the war, ersatz coffee made from acorns, roasted barley and oats, the flavour enhanced with coal tar.

Tea was made from the blooms on the linden tree mixed with beech buds. Cakes were made from flour from horse chestnuts adding whatever was to hand, honey, or plums and topped with delicious looking ersatz cream made from chemicals and tasting of absolutely nothing! Meat was almost unobtainable and ingenuity prevailed to create a lamb chop lunch. Rice was well cooked and moulded into the shape of a chop, a wooden skewer inserted to resemble the bone, fried in mutton tallow, served with peas, a sprig of watercress, and the finishing touch, a paper rosette atop the "bone".

Miss Stout was at pains to warn us of the resourcefulness of this still dangerously powerful people who are concentrating every effort on recapturing their lost trade. The British Zone Review of 1918 agrees that the Germans "are only shamming dead economically and financially and exploiting the situation to arouse sympathy."

Anne concluded her talk with these thoughts.

The fact that our homes are inviolate, secure, is due to the living wall which stood between ourselves and a ruthless foe. To the majority of soldiers King and Country were somewhat vague ideals to fight for, but "home" was a tangible reality, a little world of its own to be protected even if it meant the laying down of life itself. If home was so much worth dying for, surely it ought to be worth living for in the peaceful years to come. The German women know this and have strained every resource to keep a home intact for their returning warriors. They realise, as we are slow to do, that every soldier that has been under fire, has got a severe shock to his nervous system; is more or less a case of shell shock, and requires good nourishing food, plenty of rest, absence of domestic worries and excitement if he is to be brought back to his normal state. This is the task of the home maker, present and future for the sake of the war weary men who have returned, and in gratitude to the memory of those who sleep in the sunlit gardens of France and Flanders.

I believe that Anne had been planning since August 1915 to visit the battlefields if ever an opportunity arose.

Sgt. David Webster Irvine aged 31 years, a volunteer with the Liverpool Pal's Battalion, was reported missing in August 1915 at the battle of Verdun. David and Anne had planned to marry when the war was over. David's father was Captain David Irvine of Liverpool. Anne and David's parents were second cousins and the families had visited each other over the years. Charlie caught a moment on camera at the dining room table in the Medical Hall, just before the war; David and Anne, hands entwined, drinking a toast to their future together.

In 1920 there was public discussion as to whether it was appropriate to hold Up-Helly-A' so soon after the war. Anne responded to *The Shetland Times* in a very positive way. "Personally I do not think we can do too much to help the boys who are left to forget their dreadful yesterdays". She wrote the following verse which was published in *The Shetland Times*, January 1920.

Up-Helly-A'

The last long war is ended, now the waves of peace we tread,
Our grand old flag, unsullied yet, floats proudly overhead.
Now resurrect our ancient rite, for five years lain aside,
And let Up-Helly-A' be held, with all its old time pride.

But five long years have left a gap, one cannot bridge at will,
And there were those, who with us marched, whose gallant hearts are still.
Who reared aloft the flaming torch, and fed the dragons pyre,
Un witting their Valhalla, with its baptism of fire.

Oh battlefields of Flanders, O wasted land of France,
From o'er the Northern waters, blows this breath of wild romance.
It stirs among your shattered trees, and ruined cities fair,
And moans its way amidst the sea, of crosses small and bare.

Your grey old town beside the sea, is missing you tonight,
For younger hands than yours must learn, to hold the torch upright.
And those who fought beside you, the merry dance will tread,
You would not have it otherwise, O unforgotten dead.

A.E.S. Lerwick
January 1920.

We find Anne writing again at the bequest of *The Shetland Times*. "A short verse for Armistice Day 1921".

Armistice Day 1921.

Rosemary for remembrance and laurels for the brave,
But for our Empires honoured Dead, what homage do we crave?
A little space of silence, the world's grief to share.
Within the heart humility, and on the lip a prayer.

A.E.S. 11th November, 1921.

In 1922 Anne married Sgt. David Irvine's brother, John, and travelled with him to live in China where he was in business, and where their eldest son was born. They named him David.

Anne Elizabeth Stout, 1919.

Anne and colleague at the counter of the Church Army Hut, Lerwick.

Anne with colleague outside Church Army Hut in Lerwick.

Cologne 1919. Anne seated to right of the adopted dog.

Anne (right) with fellow workers and soldiers outside the club in Cologne.

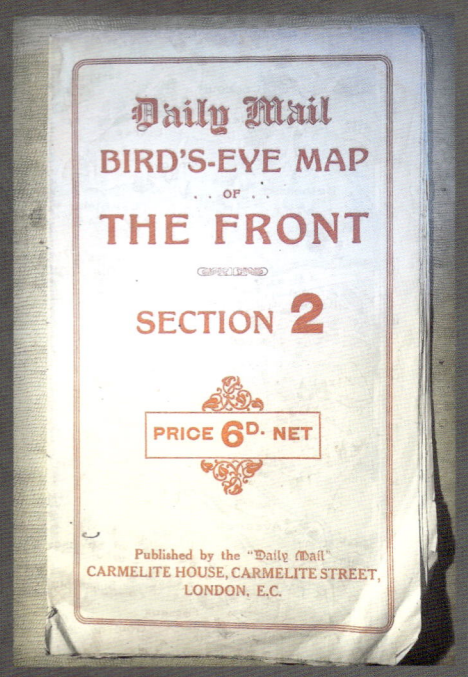

Daily Mail Bird's-Eye Map of The Front used by Anne.

Cologne. Fort Bocklemunt Anti-aircraft Battery.

LONDON
England
English Channel
Folkestone
Dover
Calais
Dunkerque
BELGIAN ARMY
Nieuwpoort
Ostende
Zeebrugge
Holland
Antwerp
Belgium
BRUSSELS
IMPERIAL GERMAN ARMY
Ypres
Lille
Armentières
St. Omer
Lens
Vimy
Arras
BRITISH ARMY
Cambrai
Le Cateau
Mons
Albert
Amiens
River Somme
St Quentin
Maubeuge
Namur
River Meuse
Liège
River Rhine
Koblenz
Charleville
Mézières
IMPERIAL GERMAN ARMY
FRENCH ARMY
Le Havre
Compiègne
Soissons
River Aisne
River Oise
Chantilly
Reims
Verdun
River Seine
PARIS
Château Thierry
River Marne
St Mihiel
FRENCH ARMY
U.S. ARMY (1918)
France
Luxembourg
Metz
IMPERIAL GERMAN ARMY
Nancy
Toul
River Meurthe
St Dié
River Meuse
Épinal
River Moselle
FRENCH ARMY
Colmar
Mulhouse
Belfort
Pfetterhouse
Western Front Battlefields 1914-1918
Battle Front June 1916
General Headquarters Allied Armies
General Headquarters German Army
Fortified Town
N

The ruins of the famous library at the University of Louvain. *N.J. Boon*

Visitors surveying the remains of the
Great Medieval Cloth Hall Ypres 1919.

Poelcappelle (the road from Langemarck to Dixmude)
with abandoned British tank as described by Anne.

Passchendaele, 1919. *Canada at War*

Road to Passchendaele, 1919. *Canada at War*

Acknowledgement of service from The Scottish Churches' Huts.

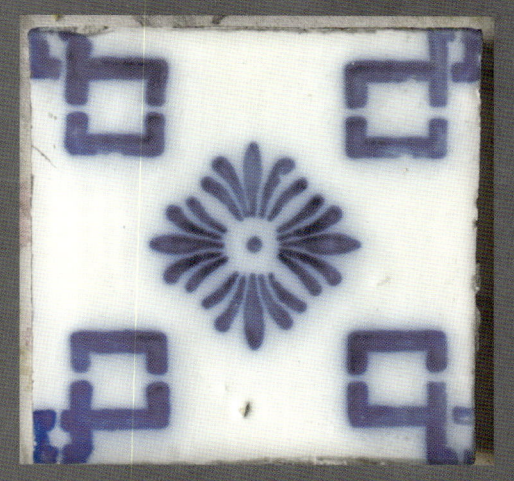

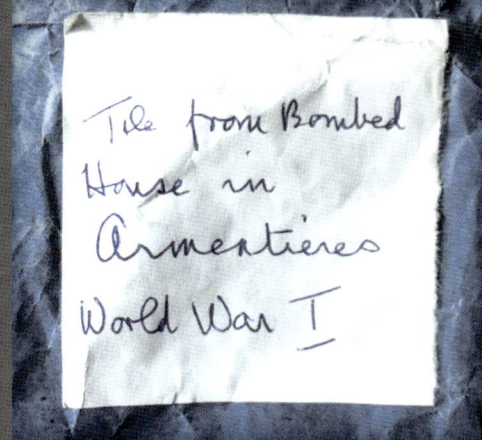

The tile picked up by Anne from a bombed house in Armentieres with Anne's inscription on the back confirming its authenticity.

The shell cases given to Anne at Armentiers.

Elizabeth with Margaret (left) and Harriet (right)
in their new wet weather attire and leather boots, c 1911.

Elizabeth Brown Stout 1890-1973

The Years Before the War

Elizabeth was born in the Medical Hall Lerwick in 1890, the second child of Margaret and Charles Brown Stout. She was educated at the Anderson Educational Institute and later attended Moray House Training College in Edinburgh, at a time when careers for women, especially from the remote Shetland Islands, were in their infancy.

Betty, as she was always known, took a lead in the artistic and literary life of the town, and encouraged her siblings to follow. She was among the first to write poetry and plays in the Shetland dialect which were performed in the town by her sisters and their friends. Her work was greatly appreciated judging by the applause and the calls for "encore! encore!" often a witty poem in dialect which brought the house down. The girls were not allowed to speak dialect at home, but Betty, who had a deep love for all things Shetland, wanted to show that there was a place for the rich Shetland dialect in literature.

Betty had mastered "schoolroom" French but wanted to improve her conversational French, so she encouraged her sisters to speak French at mealtimes. The girls thought this very exotic and entered into the spirit of the ploy. She was longing to visit France.

Betty was a champion for women's education and standing in society. It was not for nothing that she was affectionately known as "Betty Brown, the boss of the town!" The reading room on the Esplanade was very much a male domain. Women never ventured beyond the portals. One day Betty announced, "women can read too" and taking her sister Margaret with her, marched to the reading room and entered through the hallowed doors to be met with much rustling of newspapers. After that women went regularly to read the papers.

In 1912 Elizabeth Stout was appointed headmistress of Hamnavoe School, Burra Isle, and her sister Anne Stout was appointed assistant teacher. This suited them perfectly. They complemented each other and worked closely together to introduce "after school activities", unheard of at that time. They organised a "cairding" (preparation of raw wool for spinning) one evening for the girls, the boys were invited later for supper which the girls, assisted by the teachers, had prepared. The boys brought their fiddles and soon everyone was dancing merrily around the schoolroom.

Betty was a serious amateur archaeologist, and in 1912 was awarded the Chalmers Jervise Essay Prize by the Society of Antiquaries of Scotland for her essay entitled, "Some Shetland Brochs and Standing Stones" illustrated with her own drawings and watercolours. She had passionately researched the subject in the field, in libraries, and with her friend and mentor Jessie Saxby.

The following year James Fullerton, a fisherman who lived on Burra Isle was getting married. Betty was asked to help dress the bride, an honour accorded to the headmistress. In his youth James had found a gold bracelet imbedded in the soil on the island of Oxna, and had given it to his bride to wear on their wedding day. Unfortunately, the bride's hand was too large, but Betty, on seeing the bracelet for the first time, and hearing of its origin, asked if she might wear it to the festivities. She slipped it on her wrist. She now had the opportunity to study the "bracelet" which she was convinced was of Norse origin. I like to think of the gold armlet on her wrist, shining in the lamp light, while Betty danced the night away.

She decided to consult her friend the Shetland historian, Dr Gilbert Goudie. He agreed with Betty that the "bracelet" was of Norse origin, and with the owner's permission, took it to the National Museum of Scotland, where it was confirmed that it was indeed a gold Norse armlet of national significance.

James Fullerton was approached and agreed to sell the armlet for £20 to the National Museum of Scotland where it has pride of place among the treasures of the nation.

The Society of Antiquaries of Scotland unanimously recommended that Miss Elizabeth Stout be elected a Corresponding Member of the Society in recognition of her two outstanding achievements. Women were not permitted to become full members.

While Betty and Anne were teaching on Burra Isle legislation was passed requiring all skippers to hold a certificate of navigation and seamanship. The skippers of the Burra Isle fishing fleet were aghast and before long the teachers were consulted. Betty and Anne decided, at their own expense, and in the school holidays, to take navigation and sea craft examinations themselves, at the Central School in Lerwick. Thus prepared, they were qualified to tutor their skipper students for the forthcoming examinations.

The evening classes in navigation and seamanship were a great success and all the "students" passed the examinations, bar one who was found to be colour blind. To celebrate, the now fully qualified skippers took their teachers on a voyage around the island and back to Hamnavoe for a grand high tea prepared by their wives. The skippers never forgot the dedication of these two sisters and presents of halibut and lobster, which were not then commercial, were frequently found on their doorstep.

The sisters liked to return to Lerwick for the weekend, weather permitting. But getting back to Burra involved a very early rise on Monday morning, a walk or bicycle ride to Quarff to catch the mail boat to Trondra, a walk across Trondra to catch the mail boat to Mid Isle, Burra, and a last walk to Hamnavoe. A walk of approximately eight miles. Not for the faint hearted!

Betty Stout was considered somewhat unconventional by her contemporaries, who else would have chosen to have a studio photograph taken of herself and two younger sisters in their wet weather attire which had recently been purchased from a store in London. She was an independent woman, generous with her talents, kind and inclusive of others, but above all she was passionate for all things Shetland.

Gold Norse armlet found on the Isle of Oxna, Shetland.

Elizabeth at the wheel of the SS *Earl* on her way to Unst.

Elizabeth and sister Margaret in the drawing room of the Medical Hall.

Elizabeth with her class in the Scalloway school, 1915. The little girl is holding one of her sister Queenie's dolls.

Shetland Museum and Archives

THE LATE JAMES LAURENSON, R.N.R., BURRA ISLE.

AN APPRECIATION BY E. STOUT, HAMNAVOE.

It was with feelings of the deepest regret that the little community out here in our island home forced themselves to believe at last that no hope could be entertained for the safety of any of the crew of the ill-fated armed yacht "Viknor" which was supposed to have been lost recently off the Irish coast, with her complement of two hundred and ninety two souls. No one could throw any light on the way in which the vessel met her fate, and the Admiralty announced that she may have struck a mine, have been torpedoed, or have foundered in a gale.

Among the crew was James Laurenson of Burra Isle, and in him we mourn one of our best and bravest. Tall, straight, manly, fair-headed and blue eyed, always with a smile on his face and a cheery word for everyone— his presence among us was a very inspiration, and his loss a thing most keenly felt. His was a nature eminently loveable and kindly, helpful and gentlemanly; he was a true friend, and a dutiful and affectionate son and brother.

James was a sailor with a true sailor's love of the sea, and understanding of her ways. Born in November, 1882, he went to the fishing in due course of time, as all our men do here, and won golden opinions by his steadiness and skill. Later, the call of the seas afar and climes unknown claimed him, and he became a sailor to distant lands and peoples. His seaman's discharge book lies before me as I write, and I read of voyages to the Baltic, to the Black Sea, to the sunny Mediterranean, to the River Plate, to Chantenay, to Colombo, to Bahia, and many other places, following in bewildering succession. How we think now of his yarns, after the Evening Classes had finished for the night, when he told us of the hard work in the chains, going up the shallow Indian rivers, heaving the lead every minute or so, of the joy of steering a good ship through slapping seas when you were homeward bound, or of the vagaries of nigger cooks and Scotch engineers aboard! James' spells of deep sea sailing were varied by summers at home when he was among his islesmen going to the herring fishing. He was one of the crew of the Henrietta, LK. 1,092, when her skipper was drowned along with three other fishermen in going to Scalloway in a small boat on their way to join the large boat, some few years ago. By going to Scalloway with fate which overtook them. His last voyage to foreign places was made in the "Cairnross," of Newcastle, in 1913, and owing to an accident sustained in that ship by falling down an open hatchway into the hold and getting his head badly cut, he had to be sent to hospital. On recovering from this he came home, and spent the winter in Burra. He joined our Evening Classes in Hamnavoe as a pupil, and was a valued and useful member of the Seacrafts and Navigation classes. Being an expert in signalling he rendered yeoman service in that department, and his wide knowledge of knotting, splicing, and all branches of seamanship was often in demand, and help was always most willingly given. He made a fine model lead-line for use in the school, and also sewed a canvas bag to hold the school signalling flags. I cannot forget one evening when he showed us how the rescusitation of the apparently drowned should be done, and it was only then that we learned that he had saved two lives from the hungry sea; in one case he had to work for a long time in wet clothes at the half drowned man after diving for him in a dirty Italian harbour, before he was restored to life. At the close of the Navigation Class, James passed the Board of Trade examination in Lerwick for skipper of drifter, trawler, or other fishing vessel, and also passed an examination in signalling and had an endorsement for the latter made on his ticket. Here I may quote from a letter received the other day from one who had seen him at the Lerwick examination. "I was so sorry to hear that your very bright Laurenson man—the signaller—had laid his ashes on the altars of his gods. Poor chap, how I envy him! Here's me too old and useless when my country is in the throes of death or a new birth, and I'm only doing work any old women could do, if she would." It makes us glad to think that our appreciation is also shared by outsiders.

Last spring James joined the motor fishing boat Victory, of Burra, and proceeded to Mallaig to fish herring along the West Coast of Scotland.

Some years previously he had joined the Royal Naval Reserve and, on the outbreak of war, the boat proceeded to Lerwick. He remained on drill there, varied by a spell of work at Bressay as lookout man on the Wart hill, and then went to Portsmouth with the draft of R.N.R. men from Lerwick. After going through a course of gunnery at Whale Island and becoming a leading seaman and chief gunner, James was drafted on to the Viknor, which was commissioned at Portsmouth in December last. She went to South Shields, which port she left on 7th January for Liverpool, and nothing has since been heard of her. Some bodies and wreckage from the ship have been washed ashore on the coast of Antrim, but as yet, no identification of our islesman's body has taken place. But as time goes on, and the silence lengthens, we feel in our hearts that he has crossed the bar and met his Pilot face to face at last. Brave in duty always, we are sure that he did not flinch when the end came, but that he looked steadfastly into the unknown in the sure hope that afterwards there would be "no more sea." When the Evening School again started this winter, although on duty, James joined the Navigation Class in Lerwick, and, after being sent to Portsmouth, did not forget us in Hamnavoe, for he sent us a card wishing our classes all success. Knowing our interest in signalling, the card he chose to send bore a facsimile of Nelson's famous signal "England expects every man this day will do his duty" in coloured flags. May that message be as a clarion call to-day reminding us that it is only by doing our duty by our beloved country in high resolve, in brave purpose, in noble action like his, that his death can now be avenged.

War obituary written by Elizabeth, 1915. Written in the genre of the time.

Elizabeth in the uniform of the Croix Rouge Francais. France 1917.

Elizabeth Brown Stout 1890-1973

The War Years

In 1915 Elizabeth and Anne Stout resigned from their teaching posts on Burra Isle in favour of the mainland; Elizabeth to the school in Scalloway and Anne to the Central School in Lerwick. The war was dominating life in Lerwick and they wanted to be at the heart of the Shetland war effort.

Anne and Betty soon found themselves being approached by grieving friends to write obituaries for their loved ones killed in the war, a particularly sad task when they recognised the names of their former navigation students.

Anne could now devote all her spare time to the Church Army Hut at Alexandra Wharf, the Missions to Seamen Hut and Queen Mary's Needlework Guild (QMNG). Betty wrote plays and verse for fundraising concerts, performed by her sisters and their friends. She was very artistic and designed and made eye catching posters for a "Gifts Day for Servicemen" organised by QMNG. Anne wrote the patriotic verbal appeal that accompanied the posters. They worked well together and complemented each other's talents. Betty, however, was quietly making plans of a more adventurous nature.

Betty had made contact with the Oxford Suffrage Society who had put political aspirations aside and established the "Oxford Women's Canteens" in France. Early in the war an Oxford tutor on vacation in France had been appalled at the lack of provision for the French Poilus (soldier) on his way to and from the front. On her return to Oxford she publicised this sad state of affairs, a fund was started by a group of like-minded women and discussions were held with the Croix Rouge Francaise. As a result, a canteen was opened near Dormans on the Marne. The canteen was situated outside the town beside a large army camp near the railway line, a stopping place for soldiers before the Reims' front. Betty wrote expressing an interest to join the group and work in one of their canteens. She travelled to Oxford to meet the group where she must have made a good impression because she was soon on her way to France. The work was voluntary and all expenses were funded by the women themselves.

Betty arrived in Dormans via Paris on the main line from Paris to Reims, which now ended at Dormans, the rail beyond having been destroyed. She was met by one of the canteen workers who escorted Betty to her lodgings with a widow in the town, but all meals were to be taken in the canteen.

The canteen was a large hut with long tables down the length of the room and another table across one end for the great pots of coffee and hot chocolate. Behind was the kitchen presided over by a capable French woman, who prepared the main meals of the day, and two plantons (orderlies), two cheery old soldiers, who fetched and carried and did the washing-up. Most of the provisions for the canteen such as pâté, meat and bread were bought in the little town. They foraged further afield to outlying farms to buy fresh fruit, vegetables and eggs. Betty enjoyed these excursions which gave her an opportunity to talk with the farmers and their wives, and enjoy the beauty of the low hills with swathes of white lily of the valley and blue iris. There were cherry orchards and vineyards and it was only the distant rumble of gunfire that reminded one of the war.

One day, not long after she arrived, Betty was out foraging at a nearby farm when she caught sight of a long line of khaki clad British soldiers marching towards the line, while a long line of blue-grey French soldiers carrying their possessions, were marching away from the line, and towards Dormans and the canteen.

Since the almost complete destruction of Reims this sector was considered quiet, although the front line trenches had to be held. The British soldiers, weary from the Somme, were being sent to this quieter sector for a rest and to give the French soldiers some relief. Betty flew back to the canteen which was for some time a swirl of khaki and grey-blue, and English and French voices.

A few days later Betty and the other workers were relaxing after supper, when they saw a train on the temporary line arriving with open trucks crowded with women and children "our hearts sank, refugees, this could only mean one thing, the Germans were advancing". The Germans were indeed advancing in overwhelming numbers and destroying everything in their path. This was the German spring offensive of 1918.

> All night the refugees came, mostly old people, women and children, with their pet animals and their most treasured possessions. When the trains were destroyed, they walked; exhausted, hungry and frightened. The soldiers in the camp were splendid and gave up their beds and the canteen workers fed them with what food they had. Most left on an early morning train from Dormans.
>
> The next day was a nightmare. Two of the workers and one of the plantons set off with the wheelbarrow to buy all the provisions available in the town in preparation for whoever may come, and returned with meat, and all the available pate and bread.

The French cook did not turn up, but the two plantons did, and cooked splendidly. We made coffee and hot chocolate and bouillon and never had time to stir from the canteen. The stream of refugees were now joined by wounded British soldiers all miserable and exhausted. They had hardly arrived in the sector when the enemy began to advance, and half of their possessions had not followed them. They were worn out from their previous retreat and the whole strength of the German army seemed to be against them. Our men were retreating hopelessly. They had lost their officers, no one to direct them, or tell them where to make a stand.

The canteen was full to overflowing with men wounded or so exhausted they could barely ask for food. The atmosphere was one of total confusion and despair. When we at last got to our hut we found English women from another canteen which had been destroyed, and nurses who had lost everything, and were attending to stretcher cases which were lying everywhere. During the night the wounded were put on the last train to leave Dormans.

The next day there was no meat or bread to buy and most shops were closed. We found the commandant and told him that we would be closing the canteen for lack of food and although he knew, he did not tell us, that the town was to be evacuated. We went to our lodgings at night where everything was prepared for us as usual, but our landlady had gone. It was a queer feeling to be left in an empty town.

The next day an English RAMC[1] unit turned up, commandeered our hut and prepared a first class dinner of beef for the colonel and his men and invited us to join them. We had a merry meal! And all the time aeroplanes were circling over us and the noise was terrific. A few stray refugees and soldiers passed through during the day, but we realised our usefulness here was over. The colonel quietly told us that the Germans were advancing, there was nothing more for him to do in Dormans, so he would be leaving as soon as he was ready, taking us with him. It was a great relief to know that he would be in charge of our retreat.

On the advice of the colonel the canteen workers packed up their personal possessions and waited at the roadside for the colonel's motor vehicles. "We can take more luggage than that" and told his men to "to go and fetch the other things" so in the end, ourselves and all our possessions were packed into the vehicles as dawn was breaking. A few soldiers were waiting to blow up the bridge, and that done our spirits rose as we drove through the freshness of a new day towards Paris.

But what cheered us most were the British troops we passed going towards the enemy. They seemed amazed to see us and grinned and waved as we cheered and clapped them on their way.

---

1   RAMC – Royal Army Medical Corps.

Betty's sister Margaret received a short note from her written as they were leaving Dormans and posted in Paris.

> The enemy are only two kilometres from our place and everyone hurriedly quitting – once we all get collected again we'll probably be sent somewhere further back – some nurses have come in – had lost everything – fled down – Isn't it rotten when I'd troddled the bike and tin kettles safely through.

They eventually reached Paris two days later and arrived somewhat dishevelled at the headquarters of the Croix Rouge Francaise (CRF) where they were told that hospitals were clamouring for workers, and indeed by 7am they were all at work!

The very large and prestigious Hotel Astoria had been turned into a hospital by the CRF mainly for French servicemen. It was to be administered by the French Red Cross, whilst the nursing was directed by the English Red Cross, and all the nurses were English! The hotel had been acquired by the British banker Herbert Stern 1st Baron Michelham in 1914, to be used as a hospital for British servicemen.

The Oxford women found rooms at the YWCA Hostel where they slept, all meals and time being spent at the hospital. Each floor in the hotel was assigned to a particular ward and was made up of a number of small rooms, requiring more nurses than normal to care for the patients.

The matron gave the Oxford women personal instruction during the first week, to enable them to start their nursing careers as probationers. Betty adapted quickly to her new role resplendent in the uniform of the CRF, her fluent French was a considerable advantage and she was assigned to a ward for the Poilus, French soldiers.

The Germans were advancing on Paris and all women and children who could travel, were sent from the capital, and those allowed to stay, such as themselves, were registered and told what to do in the event of a sudden evacuation. Betty writes:

> Our method of escape appears to be undecided. However, one of our team who is learning to drive, has promised to take us all out of Paris by car. Some think it might be safer to stay!
>
> It was a very strange Paris. The streets were almost deserted and all the public monuments were covered with sandbags. We didn't mind, we were far too busy and got on well together in our YWCA digs. After a good dinner at the Astoria we had tea and biscuits at the "digs" which grew into supper parties. I made marmalade, which we all missed, mixed in the wash hand basin and cooked over my little stove. It was eaten greedily at breakfast. We had liberal rations from our military food cards and bread coupons, so were never hungry.

Paris was under siege. Air raid sirens wailed mournfully day and night. From March to August 1918 Paris was under bombardment from the Paris Gun. The German long range siege gun, the largest piece of artillery used during the war, a super gun with a range of 81 miles! The gun was mounted on a turntable on a train, it was too large and heavy to be transported any other way. The shells fell at 15 minute intervals as the mammoth gun revolved on its turntable and did considerable damage to Paris. On Good Friday, March 1918, a single shell hit the roof of St Gervais et St Protais Eglaise, the roof collapsed on the congregation, 91 were killed and 68 injured.

Betty wrote a note to her sister Margaret from Paris in June 1918.

> Got practically no sleep last night in Paris as there was a raid so you can imagine it, everyone got up and went to the basement, then at ¼ to seven the Paris Gun began a bombardment awful bangs as shells fell.

The letter ends:

> Never leet (tell) at home but as I am writing in bed at 9pm the Paris Gun has begun again AWFUL bang quite near. Next bang won't be so bad as it turns round so I'll be O.K. now for the rest of the night. Best love (sleepily) Lil.

Betty got on well with the Poilus and talked to them about their families and home life. She increased her vocabulary in a new direction, picking up the soldiers "slang" which she found useful when scolding boisterous patients. Those recovering from shell shock were often unaware of what they were doing when they rampaged around the ward. It took all the nurse's strength and persuasion to get the patient back into bed, sometimes the Polius imagined she was the enemy and lashed out, or that she was their mother or wife and tried to kiss her!

The daily routine of bed making and washing was often protracted when some Poilus behaved like naughty schoolboys teasing the "English nurses", but Betty, after years of teaching country boys in Shetland, was

French Bread coupons, 1918.

quite able to deal with the situation which usually ended in laughter. The patients needed constant attention, meals were served and several patients fed, they assisted the nurses to change dressings and "ticketed" new arrivals. Bed pans were in constant demand. Ward work was relentless. At the end of the day they were exhausted. This was the time of the big push by the enemy and wounded French soldiers were being brought in by the hour. Paris was expected to fall.

In 1950 Aunt Betty took me to Paris and we spent a month visiting her old haunts and journeying further afield to the Argonne where she spent time after the armistice. She took me to the Hotel Astoria in Paris, which was now the headquarters of the American Army. We paused in the palatial entrance hall, and having introduced herself to the officer in charge, she described the scene vividly, as she remembered it in 1918. The Americans were spellbound.

> It was night and blackout. The Paris gun was wrecking havoc overhead, a few candles and lamps gave a flickering light to the horrific scene as stretcher bearers struggled in with their terrible loads. The wounded Poilus had come straight from the front, their wounds were terrible, many wounded dangerously in several places. That great enemy gas gangrene was already present and surgeons worked desperately to save lives.
>
> Most of the poor fellows were too far gone to say much, uniform in shreds and everything caked in mud and gore. The floor was soon covered with stretchers, and as soon as they had been carried off new arrivals took their place. Those that were not on stretchers sat on the great marble staircase and soon the whole staircase was a mass of wounded men. We were putting swabs on terrible wounds, administering drinks, sending them off to the x-ray room and theatre. Everything had to be done in a tearing hurry as surgeons fought to save lives. The stench was terrible.
>
> In the ward we removed and ticketed the blood and mud stained clothing for washing, and emptied out the pockets with some curious finds – small tins of food, religious icons, letters, photographs, and on one occasion a loaded revolver! The men were usually so exhausted that they fell asleep even while having their dressings done. At times like this we were at the beck and call of the nurses and doctors, bringing basins of water, swabs, dressings, and then clearing the blood and gore away. And all the time we could hear shells exploding and now and again the building shuddered.
>
> It was an awful time. At last the great good news came. The enemy advance had been stopped. Paris was saved. The enemy retreated, people returned to Paris and resumed war time life again. The casualties continued to pour in and we probationers were kept as busy as ever.
>
> I didn't mind night duty it was usually quiet, once everyone had their medicines,

and drinks, except for the air raids, when the walking patients took themselves down to the basement, and we had to decide if the stretcher cases were to be carried down. They always objected and would rather stay where they were. Lights had to be extinguished and little night lights took their place. Air raids were fairly constant at this time and the high windows provided a spectacular view. We were given bread and butter and two eggs to keep us going through the night, and then we had eggs with our petite dejeuner before we went home to sleep.

Betty was now living in Paris. Armed with her Baedeker[2] she explored Paris, the famous buildings and museums, art galleries and gardens, and it wasn't long before she was introduced to the British Army and Navy Leave Club in the Place de la Republique. The club was started by Lady Decima Moore, the English singer and actress, and the Rev. A.S.U. Blunt, in a magnificent Paris mansion lent by Baron D. Erlanger and staffed by 45 enthusiastic volunteers. The club was set up to help servicemen spend their leave time as pleasantly and profitably as possible. All free of charge.

Leave was a contentious issue. Soldiers were allowed leave every 15 months. Officers every three months. This led to a huge press campaign for more equal and regular leave time. From 1915 the British Army gradually allowed fighting men to take a few days leave at the rear, and many choose to spend it in Paris.

The club was a huge success. In the two years it was open, 59,000 men registered and 700,000 meals were served. As well as free accommodation and meals, the club provided free entertainment which included guided tours of Paris and Versailles. Betty was soon invited to join the band of guides and nothing pleased her more than being able to share her love of Paris with others. Little was she to know that this decision would change her life.

Her years of teaching experience and public speaking stood her in good stead for shepherding groups of boisterous Tommies around Paris. She could deal with petty French officials in their own vernacular, which she had learnt from the Poilus, much to the soldiers delight.

Betty had taken a group of soldiers to Versailles and was giving her customary introductory talk, when an American naval lieutenant asked if he might join the group. She, probably encouraged by the soldiers, agreed. As the tour progressed Lieut. Nathan Levy was captivated by this vivacious intelligent young woman, who held her soldiers spellbound with stories of romance and intrigue at the Palace of Versailles.

The tour over, Betty was shepherding the last of her soldiers into the large powerful automobiles belonging to the club, when Lieut. Levy approached her to

---

2   A Baedeker was any of the series Guide Books to Europe produced by the German publisher Karl Baedeker 1801-1859 or his company.

say how much he had enjoyed the tour and would she join him for dinner at the club that evening? She enjoyed the dinner and the attention and agreed that he could join her on her next tour to Notre Dame and the Isle de la Cité.

    The Armistice came like a bolt from the blue! Rumours of a peace incentive had been circulating for some time, but we only had a broad perspective of the war from newspapers which were heavily censored. Our Poilus took the news calmly, the wounded began to recover hourly as happiness spread throughout the hospital. At first it was the silence. Then we could hear cheering outside and we opened the windows and joined in!

An official radio announcement was made from Paris at 6.01am on the 11th November, 1918.

    Marshal Foch to the Commander-in-Chief
1. Hostilities will be stopped on the entire front beginning at 11 o'clock Nov 11th (French hour)
2. The Allied troops will not go beyond the line reached at that hour on that date until further notice.

    Signed
    Marshal Foch 5.45 am.

    Betty continued nursing at the Astoria until her patients returned to their homes or were moved to an established hospital. She continued to take groups of Tommies – now in exuberant mood – around Paris and Versailles, and her friendship with Lieut. Levy blossomed.

    The period after the armistice was tense as people adjusted to peace. The German army was given a short period to withdraw behind the German border and the victorious armies became the armies of occupation.

    Italy had entered the war on the side of the Entente in 1915. In April 1918 the Italian Prime Minister, Orlando, ordered Italian soldiers to France, commanded by Alberico Albricci in order to show his support for the Triple Entente.

    In mid-May the Italian soldiers were sent to the Argonne for training, then to the Reims Salient where they fought in the Second Battle of the Marne, 15th July – 2nd August, suffering heavy casualties. In September the Corps was moved to the River Aisne south of Soupir and there it stayed; fighting along the Chemin des Dames continuing to push the Germans north until the war ended. The conditions of the Armistice gave Germany 14 days to evacuate all remaining occupied territory and German territory claimed by France and Belgium, and 28 days to withdraw its armed forces across the Rhine. The Italian army was following close on their heels towards Luxembourg which the Germans had occupied during the war, and which they were speedily evacuating under the terms of the armistice.

You may wonder what all this has to do with Elizabeth Brown Stout! The Croix Rouge Francaise wanted two workers to manage their canteen for the Italian Army. They suggested to Betty and her co-worker, Myfanwy Rhys, that they might like to volunteer for this work. It was an interesting and exciting challenge for our two intrepid volunteers, who packed their bags and set off for Luxembourg and the headquarters of the Italian Army, now under French High Command.

Myfanwy Rhys of Jesus College Oxford was a leading suffragette in Oxford. She was the daughter of Sir John Rhys, first Professor of Celtic Studies at Oxford and fellow of Jesus College. He was an influential and important figure in wider culture and society. Betty and Myfanwy, two like-minded women, had formed a close friendship in Paris.

The Croix Rouge Francaise had located an empty shop in an area which had escaped war damage, and here Myfanwy and Betty set up their canteen. They decorated the entrance with Union Jacks and Italian flags, and a welcome sign. "Foyer - Cantine des Dames Anglaise." They displayed more flags which could be easily seen by the Italian soldiers looking for their canteen. The idea of a canteen for soldiers was something new to the Italian army, and two soldiers immediately volunteered to help with any heavy work, such as drawing water and carrying fuel for the stoves. The interior was dark and gloomy, so Betty and Myfanwy set about with paint, paper and more flags to brighten the room. The old wooden shop counter made an excellent stand for the urns of coffee and pots of hot chocolate. They also served soup and bread and sold cigarettes. The coffee they served was made from the used coffee grounds from the officer's mess. They complained and were given new coffee to mix with the used grounds to make a more palatable brew. Betty, of course, had her small portable stove and tea pot with her and made pancakes which were very popular with the soldiers.

Betty and Myfanwy were thrilled to find they were serving with General Garibaldi's famous "Brigata Alpi". The general was a grandson of the famous General Giuseppe Garibaldi (1807-1882) the Italian soldier and nationalist leader. He took a keen personal interest in the canteen. He was intrigued by these two educated and cultured women who were giving up their time to dispense refreshments to his soldiers!

Betty and Myfanwy explored the surrounding battlefields in their free time. They held the rank of officer which entitled them to free 1st class travel on the railway, if any trains could be found. Betty told her sister Margaret of this strange encounter and she wrote it down in her diary at the time.

They ran a small canteen for the soldiers – mostly coffee for the soldiers. They used to let each other off to go trips to see the war zones, but the railway lines were very broken up. They had to go to the Italian headquarters to get a pass signed for these expeditions and on one occasion Betty was confronted by a military figure behind a desk with penetrating eyes. He asked if she would meet him next day as he wanted to perfect his English – would she teach him? She declined to the man's annoyance. She kept the pass because there was a map of the area on the back of it and years later, when she looked at it, she saw that the pass was signed "Benito Mussolini". This was Betty's story. This was January 1919.

When I was in France in 1950 with Aunt Betty she took me to the area she and Myfanwy had explored soon after the Armistice. She described the Chemin des Dames (the Ladies Path) the scene of so much fighting and where the Italian army had harried the retreating Germans back to Germany. She explained the origin of the curious name the "Ladies Path". It was the most direct route taken by two daughters of Louis XV, Adelaide and Victoire, from Paris to the Chateau de Boves where they were frequent visitors. They would not have recognised the Chemin des Dames as described by Betty in January 1919.

The Chemin des Dames is 30 kilometres long and runs along a ridge between the Rivers Aisne and Ailette. There was miles and miles of desolate country all around, the whole countryside torn up and stripped of its trees which are only blackened remains. Trenches, barbed wire, bits of gun carriages and gas masks and water bottles and boots all trodden into the mud and here and there a bit of a cross or a hole showing a grave. Then no more trenches just shell holes some quite 30 feet deep all one great upheaval of earth. This was "no man's land.

We were often accompanied by a soldier who appeared out of nowhere and seemed glad to walk with us and tell us of a battle fought, it was as if by talking about it, they were sharing the grief they felt for their fallen comrades. It was all so recent.

Betty found a train which could take her to Dormans, she wanted to see what was left of their canteen after the Germans had invaded the area in the spring. The train struggled over the terrible torn up ground. The rails ran on planks of wood covering the shell holes and eventually ran out of fuel and to a stop. There was desolation all around, the villages they passed were just heaps of stones and debris. The train drivers got out and gathered broken wood from the remains of dwellings to stoke the engine.

Betty climbed down from the train and wandered among the ruins.

Here and there lonely graves of soldiers buried where they fell marked with a wooden cross some with names some without and some with a helmet stuck on top of a post. German and French and Italian all together in death as their mouldy clothing sank into the mud with their helmets, rucksacks and boots.

I eventually disembarked at Dormans near the remains of the army camp and made my way, skirting shell holes, to the site of our canteen. Among the debris I recognised traces of familiar objects which had once been an important part of something so good. The nearby farms where I had bought eggs were reduced to rubble. Not an animal to be seen. The fruit trees torn asunder, but pushing bravely through the torn earth, exquisite green and white snowdrops.

The train had completed its mission and I clambered back on board. The French drivers made coffee with hot water from the engine and I had some biscuits. We were all feeling the cold now the day was drawing to a close.

After the failure of the German spring offensive in 1918, political unrest broke out in Germany, leading to the downfall of the Imperial Regime, the flight of the Kaiser to Holland , and the establishment of the Weimar Republic, which in turn was challenged by left wing political agitators.

The intrepid Betty set off with her Baedeker to explore Luxembourg. The Prime Minister Paul Eyschen had died after 27 years in office and there was friction between the Grand Duchess and her government, a rebellion, and a communist insurgency. The first night she woke in her hotel room to the sound of shooting outside in the square and much shouting. She put her head under the bedclothes. The next morning everything had returned to normal! There had been an unsuccessful coup during the night and most of the populace were wearing white armbands in support of the Weimar Republic. Betty set out with her Baedeker to explore Luxembourg, as she had planned.

The canteen was a great success with the Italian soldiers. Neither Betty or Myfanwy spoke Italian, and French became the common language, but they soon found that thanks to their schoolroom Latin they could follow simple conversations in Italian. General Garibaldi took the opportunity to visit the canteen, have a cup of coffee and talk with Betty and Myfanwy. He was amazed that Betty had travelled from Shetland to help soldiers in France.

The name Garibaldi had Shetland associations for Betty. General Giuseppe Garibaldi and his 1,000 volunteers had captured Sicily and Naples in 1860 to unite with the Kingdom of Italy. The soldiers wore distinctive red shirts. The fashion in Shetland circa 1870 was for blouses made from red cotton printed with a paisley pattern, which became popularly known as your "Garibaldi".

Betty and Myfanwy were invited to return to Italy to receive medals to commemorate their services to the Italian Army Corps, but sadly due to other commitments they had to turn down the invitation. Miss Myfanwy Rhys was expected back to take up her college appointment in Oxford, and Betty's life had taken an unexpected direction. The general was very disappointed, he had been genuinely grateful for their hard work and concern for the well being of his soldiers.

Lieut. Levy was determined not to lose touch with Betty and spent his leave with her in Luxembourg. He accompanied her on one of her expeditions to the battlefields where she photographed him beside an abandoned tank. But it wasn't all gloom. Soon letters were winging their way to Shetland with the news that Betty was engaged to be married to an American officer she had met in Paris!

On the 22nd May, 1919, Miss Elizabeth Brown Stout married Lieut Nathan Levy in Paris. They were both in uniform. *The Shetland News* reported the event.

> The bride wore the becoming uniform of the French Red Cross, white linen pleated dress, white shoes and stockings, and nurse's white veil, and carried a bouquet of white roses tied with the French tri-colour, the bridegroom wore trim naval uniform. The bride's going away dress was the outdoor uniform of the French Red Cross, navy blue dress, cloak and veil. Her Maid of Honour was Miss Myfanwy Rhys and a reception was held in the British Army and Navy Leave Club.

The time had come for Betty to resign from her wartime position with the French Red Cross and return to Shetland with her husband where they received a warm welcome from astonished friends and relations.

Lieut. and Mrs Nathan Levy left Britain for the USA and a new life. And her sister Margaret went too.

The British Army and Navy Leave club in Paris.

Soupir, one of the ruined villages Betty came upon in France, 1918.

The canteen for Italian soldiers in the Tatisserie (furnishing shop). Betty and Myvanwy standing under sign "Foyer – cantine – des – dames – Anglaise".

Elizabeth on leave in Shetland. From left. Harriet, Elizabeth in uniform, a friend from Burra Isle, Margaret and their Australian cousin Jack Sinclair on leave from France, 1918.

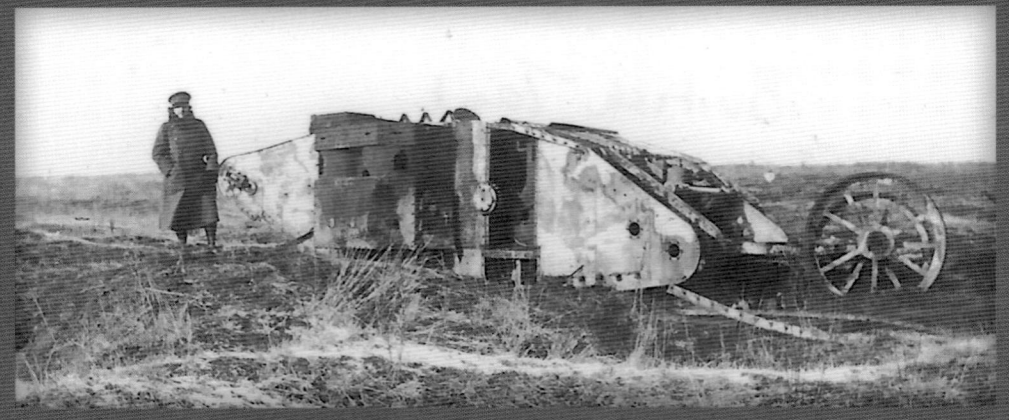

Lieut. Levy photographed by Betty on a battlefield with a British tank.

The scene of devastation after the battle of the Marne, 1918.

Wedding of Lieut. Nathan Levy USA Navy and Miss Elizabeth Brown Stout . Maid of Honour Miss Myvanwy Rhys. Paris. 1919.

Francisca Mary Stout, on the right, with her sister Margaret at college in Edinburgh 1912.

Francisca Mary Stout
1890 - 1913
The Years Before the War

Francis was tragically killed on 13th November, 1913, aged 23 years. She was returning by bicycle to Lerwick from Cunningsburgh, where she was a teacher. Just outside Lerwick she lost control on a steep brae and crashed into a concrete pillar. There had been concern that this was an accident black spot and the concrete pillar was immediately removed after the accident.

Mr and Mrs Stout and the family were overwhelmed with grief. Mr Stout wrote in his diary, "This is the saddest day of my life". Francis was an exceptional young woman, with a sweet and generous nature. Her pupils at the Cunningsburgh school were devastated. Everyone loved her.

Margaret received the news from Mrs Fordyce Clark at the digs in Edinburgh that she had shared with Francis for two years. Charlie at University in Glasgow had also received the sad news, and together they made their way to Shetland in time for the funeral.

All the schools and many shops closed. A hush fell over the town.

Margaret was inconsolable. She and Francis had always been close and spent holidays together since childhood. Sharing digs in Edinburgh with Francis and other Shetland girls had been such fun.

Francis was not as extrovert as her siblings, often seen standing at the back of an unruly group, quietly smiling. She wrote poetry and essays for publication, and was a very talented watercolour artist.

The family never got over her untimely death.

Charlie climbing on Noss, bare feet, collar and tie.

Charles Brown Stout 1891-1974

The Years Before the War

Charles Brown Stout junior was 22 years old in 1914 and as the eldest son he was expected to carry on the family business. He led a carefree and adventuresome life. He was quite a wild boy and according to his six sisters, very spoilt.

Photography held a fascination for Charlie. His first photographic album is dated 1910. Inside the cover are details of his cameras, a Sandringham No K4 and a Sandringham Folding Plate Camera. He developed and printed his own photographs in a dark room in one of the cellars under the shop. Charlie has left us a unique archive as he records the everyday activities of family and friends.

He was a skilled and fearless climber, an excellent shot, a clever game fisherman, a keen sailor, a confident swimmer and deep diver, and a member of the Vulcan Swimming Club. He was awarded the Royal Lifesaving Medal for rescuing a fellow deep diver, William Sinclair from the seabed during a Lerwick regatta. He took a prominent part in the regatta, always a strong contestant for the prize ham at the end of the greasy pole!

Charlie had formed a friendship with a Dutch sea Captain, Cornelis den Dulk who sailed between Scheveningen and Lerwick in his lugger the SCH 50. Charlie aged 18 and always ready for adventure returned to Scheveningen in the lugger with four Shetland ponies! I recently met Capt Cornelis den Dulk's grandson who presented me with a photograph of Charlie swimming off the Dogger Bank in the North Sea during that voyage to Holland!

He completed his studies at the University of Glasgow and returned to Lerwick to take up his duties in the chemist shop. He bought a dog, a Springer spaniel, Roy, who was his constant companion, loved by all the family and who was not camera shy!

Noss held a special place in Charlie's affections. Before the war he spent most weekends there and occasionally stayed for a week. James Jamieson the shepherd on Noss, and his wife Joan, made Charlie and his climbing friends very welcome. Their home became the base camp for climbing expeditions. They and their four daughters, Jessie, Maisie, Georgie and Lottie enjoyed the constant stream of visitors who usually brought contributions for the table of the hospitable Mrs Jamieson. Charlie's photographs have left us a unique picture of life on Noss, and enchanting photographs of the four girls and their dogs.

I was recently shown the Noss Visitor Book by Margaret Findlay the granddaughter of Mr James Jamieson and great niece of Mrs Stout. This precious little book is a tangible insight into the merry gatherings of friends caught up in the magic that was Noss. The Stout family kept a visitors book in the Medical Hall and introduced the idea to the Jamiesons. The Noss visitors' book opens in Charlie's handwriting on the 24th May, 1911, with "Charlie B. Stout Lerwick." Turning the pages of the book, Charlie appears to have visited Noss every weekend and occasionally stayed for a week. "The Medical Hall crowd," heralds Stouts, Mainland cousins from Bressay, and groups of Charlie's climbing friends. On the 2nd July, 1913, a group of seven climbers signed the visitors' book. Charles B. Stout, James B. Leask, James J. Laurenson, Andrew R. Moar, Walter Shewan, Laurence Gifford and James McLerson. Charlie summed up the day. "Had a splendid days climbing on good old Noss."

Charlie had a reputation as a skilled and fearless climber and the towering cliffs of Noss were a rewarding challenge. There are astonishing photographs of Charlie walking nonchalantly along narrow ledges hundreds of feet above the sea, bare feet, town clothes, and often a cigarette in hand. A memorable photograph of a vast cliff face shows two minute figures working their way along a narrow ledge. Not for the faint hearted.

Mr Jamieson or one of the elder girls had to row visitors across the Noss sound to the island. The sound was known to have a very strong and dangerous current. On one occasion Mrs Jamieson was startled when Charlie walked in unannounced, he had swum across the sound!

The Noss Visitor book provides an intriguing insight into life just before the war. An entry on 23rd August, 1913, caught my eye. A visit from the crew of the German yacht *Regina* ASV Kiel. The yacht was anchored at the south end of Lerwick Harbour and while one member of the crew stayed on board, the other six Germans trudged across Bressay to Noss, where they recorded their names in the visitors' book. Wilhelm Otto from Hamburg, Konrad Gebel from Hinterpommer, Friedel Grienauer from Vienna and Friedo Devens from Dusseldorf, Richard Schiess from Barmen and Herman von Engelman. The seventh man Karl Kruge the "bootsman" was hired crew and had remained with the yacht.

The next visitor has written underneath "Gott strafe these Huns" followed by another visitor "Hear! Hear!".

There was a degree of German spy hysteria among the population, encouraged by the press. I noticed that the yachtsmen all came from different areas in Germany. What was their connection? They were in fact members of the Kiel University Yacht Club on a yachting holiday! But I found my thoughts turning to Erskine Childer's novel *Riddle of the Sands*[1].

In the summer of 1912 Charlie and a group of pals formed the "Thule Ramblers Club" and camped in bell tents at the Sands o' Sound. Small groups of young men, friends since school days, some working, some students, liked to escape the confines of Lerwick during the summer. They camped by the sea with boats and fishing lines maintaining a communication line to Lerwick and family. Charlie's photographic legacy of jolly groups gathered round the gramophone entertaining young ladies at the weekend, leave us nostalgic for a bygone age. Charlie later bought the property at Sound and erected a wooden hut to make for more comfortable camping during the unpredictable Shetland summer. The crofter, Barbara Henderson, known as Baaby o'Sound, continued to live on the croft and make her daily milk round to Lerwick. She thoroughly enjoyed the company of these young men and the gifts they brought from town. Charlie eventually built a holiday house overlooking the beach and generously shared it with members of the extended Stout family.

He was a popular member of his Up-Helly-A' squad, but would not accept the role of Guizer Jarl, he was self conscious of his small stature and said in jest, he did not want to be remembered as the "Peerie Guizer Jarl!"

Charlie was clever and sailed through examinations. His six bossy sisters spoilt him, but "we always got Charlie to do our Latin homework". In 1914 Charlie successfully completed his studies at the University of Glasgow and headed for home and the chemist shop.

---

1   *The Riddle of the Sands*, a novel by Erskine Childers 1903. A secret service story of young Englishmen on a yachting holiday in the Fresian Islands off the coast of Germany prior to the First World War.

An enchanting photograph of Maisie, Georgie and Lottie Jamieson
at home on Noss with their dogs.

A Chorus Line! Sisters and cousin.

Charlie sailing his Shetland model
in Bressay Sound.

Charlie climbing Noup of Noss.

Charlie signed the first page of the Noss visitor book. The German crew of the yacht *Regina* from Kiel signed the Noss visitor book in August 1913.

Charlie on his motor boat.

Charlie triumphant with the ham from the end of the greasy pole. Lerwick regatta.

Charlie enjoyed posing in perilous places for a photographic opportunity.
Below the Noup of Noss!

First Thule Ramblers Camp, Sound, 1912.

The interior of the bell tent at Sound.
On the chair an Edison Wax Cylinder gramophone.

Thule Ramblers relaxing in camp in stiff collars and ties!
Charlie's canoe and dog.

The camp at Sound with hut built by Charlie.
Baaby continued to live in the croft house below.

Charlie in the Medical Hall pharmacy reflected in a mirror.

Charles Brown Stout MPS 1891-1974
The War Years

Charles Brown Stout MPS graduated from the University of Glasgow and was expected to take on the management of the chemist shop. It was 1914 and war had been declared. Everyone of a similar age was heading for France. Pharmacy was a reserved occupation and Charlie knew that not only the family business depended on him, but hundreds of servicemen in Shetland would depend on him for their medical supplies.

Mr Stout was now seventy and semi-retired. As the eldest son, Charlie had been groomed to inherit the family business which supported the household. Fortunately Charlie was a good chemist and businessman, and the shop did very well during the war years, benefitting from the influx of servicemen. He introduced all the paraphernalia of photography, cosmetics and hair products to the historic pharmacy. If Mr Stout had any reservations he kept them to himself.

Photography was one of his passions. His legacy of the war years is his unique collection of photographs of wartime Shetland which are the inspiration for this book. Permission had to be obtained from the senior naval officer to use a camera, and proofs of all photographs taken were to be submitted to him. The permit was valid for six months. I would be very surprised if Charlie ever applied for a permit, all the photographs of shipping in Lerwick harbour were taken surreptitiously from the drawing room windows and I imagine speed and subterfuge covered the rest.

When we cast our minds back to the war we tend to dwell on land battles forgetting the crucial role of the navy. At the outbreak of war the greatest resource that Britain possessed was her formidable naval strength, which ensured that troops and arms could be ferried to war zones and goods imported, even in the face of a devastating German submarine campaign. Hundreds of seamen who were members of the Royal Naval Reserve (RNR) and Royal Naval Voluntary Reserve (RNVR) were mobilised in 1914. 70% of Shetlanders on wartime service were sailors or merchant seamen. Most of the servicemen visiting the Medical Hall during the war and signing the visitors' book belonged to the RNR or RNVR and many gave the name of the ship on which they were serving.

The Allies could not win the war by combat alone, they had to destroy Germany's economy by blockading neutral ships transporting goods to Germany. The admiralty soon recognised Shetland's unique geographical position and the many sheltered voes (inlets) made it the perfect base for the blockade, and Shetland, between the North Sea and the Atlantic, became the other "front line". To enforce the blockade the admiralty formed the 10th Cruiser Squadron of regular warships and armed passenger liners. The squadron was based at Basta Voe and patrolled the north west approaches apprehending neutral ships suspected of carrying goods to Germany. The White Star Liner *Oceanic* lasted only a few weeks before being lost on the Hoevdi Rock, east of Foula, fortunately without loss of life. How could this have happened? Confusion and division between the Royal Navy and the Merchant Navy who were both in command of the great ship, appear to be responsible for a catastrophic series of errors of judgement leading to the *Oceanic* being pushed by the fast flowing flood tide onto the Hoevdi Grund. There she remained for two weeks before disappearing beneath the waves. There was a court martial but the admiralty decided on a "white wash" and both Capt. Henry Smith RNR the peace time captain, and Capt. William Slayer RN were exonerated in the national interest. Charlie had set his camera up on the Knab to take the iconic photograph of the great ship as she sailed out of Bressay Sound on her fateful voyage.

The requisitioned passenger liners proved to be unsuitable and the squadron was replaced by 24 armed merchant cruisers, crewed by 9,800 seamen. Neutral ships were stopped, searched at sea, and escorted to Lerwick harbour to report to the depot and guard ship, the light cruiser *Brilliant,* for further investigation. The chaplin on the *Brilliant* became a regular visitor to the Medical Hall where Mrs Stout introduced him to members of the clergy in Shetland.

In March 1917 the admiralty, after much deliberation, instituted the convoy system as being the safest way for several ships to sail during war time. After America joined the war, transatlantic convoys replaced the 10th cruiser squadron and Lerwick became the allies, convoy port. Vessels waiting for departure streamed into Bressay Sound and gathered to form convoys. A flotilla of destroyers and armed trawlers were always in station to escort them across the German Ocean (North Sea).

Lerwick Harbour served a variety of other functions during the war as supply base, examination port, an anchorage for the hospital ship *Berbice* in the closing years of the war and a haven for shipwrecked seafarers and refugees from conflict. A harbour for ships hunting submarines, minesweepers and mine layers, as well as fishing boats and British merchant shipping. During 1917 the tonnage passing through Bressay Sound, 4,500 vessels, was reported to be greater than any other in the United Kingdom. The drawing room windows of the Medical Hall gave Charlie an unrestricted opportunity to photograph this maritime miscellany.

German submarines were busy laying mines along the north west approaches to Shetland and the east side, endangering the base at Basta Voe and Lerwick harbour. Minesweepers were constantly at work. Their depot ship HMS *Impacable* was spotted by Charlie lying below the Medical Hall, heavy guns protruding, keeping a fatherly eye on the five minesweeping naval trawlers alongside. Convoy escorts of British destroyers lay regularly at the pier below the Medical Hall awaiting orders and Charlie's camera. He was spoilt for choice.

Two ships with unusual names caught my eye, in the visitor book, the *Ice Whale* Z1 and the *Pilot Whale* Z5. They were commissioned by the admiralty for anti-submarine patrol, based on the design of naval whalers. They were also referred to as the "hydrophone boats" equipped with microphones which were designed to be used underwater for recording or listening for underwater sounds indicating the proximity of submarines. Two members of the crew of the *Ice Whale* Peter Rosay RNVR and Fred Moses RNVR were frequent visitors to the Medical Hall. By the end of the war Britain had 38 hydrophone officers and 200 qualified listeners who were paid an extra four pence a day. How successful were the "hydrophones" in destroying German submarines? That seems to be open to question. Written in the margin of the visitor book on 10th October, 1918, "Hydrophone boats have returned" and on the 20th October a comment, "Departure of the hydrophone boats with Lieut. R. Watson" who had been a constant visitor and companion to members of the family. A sad day. Charlie had often been invited onboard where he had taken photographs of Lieut. Watson and friends.

The hospital ship for the 10th squadron, the *Berbice*, was based at Delting, but as the war progressed it was relocated to Lerwick in 1917. Officers from the *Berbice* often came to the house, C. Harvey SBS and C. Kitchener RMS were frequent visitors. Initially they came to purchase items from the chemist shop, but the visits became social occasions and Charlie was invited onboard the *Berbice* where he photographed the hospital ward.

Construction of a kite balloon base was started at Gremista in 1914 by Capt Saunders of the RAF. It was planned to have six vessels, 12 sheds, 12 balloons, and 264 staff! The balloons were to be flown from ships with lookouts suspended below to search for submarines. The appearance of the first two balloons on the pier in Lerwick in September 1917 caused quite a stir, as many people thought they were German airships! Needless to say they did not have a very long life in Shetland, destroyed two days later by rough weather. Capt. Saunders' grand scheme came to naught. Charlie captured the balloons on film from the drawing room windows, before they were destroyed. A large crowd of servicemen has gathered around the balloon on the pier, I imagine the public were kept at bay. The tethered balloon is spotted flying aloft while a convoy escort of British naval destroyers lies in wait below.

Charlie was dispensing in the chemist shop on the morning of 12th April, 1915, when a terrific explosion rocked the town shattering the shop windows. Charlie grabbed his camera and rushed out into the street to be met with a darkening sky and falling debris. A thick cloud of smoke hung over the fish quay. He hurried towards the scene of devastation meeting men staggering along the street covered with blood, and others lying on the ground with brains protruding and blood everywhere. Ten men were killed and forty injured. Despite censorship restrictions Charlie succeeded in taking several photographs of the chaotic scene.

The explosion had occurred in a store rented to the navy at the north end of Alexandra Wharf. The explosion was actually preceded by a fire which the crews of three admiralty trawlers had failed to extinguish. They had been warned to move away because there were explosives in the store. A second blast followed, the store was blown apart and dropped into the harbour some distance away. Debris was thrown far and wide, a chunk of timber was picked up at the Hoversta Farm in Bressay! A large beam landed on Brentham Place at the bottom of Harbour Street, the home of Mr and Mrs Ganson, causing considerable damage. The navy had disregarded an agreement not to store any inflammable material in the building and taken no precautions to safeguard the public in the event of an accident, and then refused to accept responsibility!

The admiralty responded to claims in a very high-handed manner. A few claims were partially met, but many not at all. After Mr Ganson, who was Convener of Zetland County Council, had completed repairs to his house, Rear Admiral Greatorex calmly commandeered the house for his residence, but refused to consider compensation for the enormous amount of damage the house had suffered. The whole affair of the explosion rumbled on until 1924 when the War Compensation Council decreed "no further payment due."

The origin of the explosion? In all probability, human error.

Charlie was out and about with his camera on the 9th August, 1917, Shetland Sphagnum Moss Day. Sphagnum moss was collected on a grand scale during the war and processed into field dressings. He captured the moment before the main working party moved off, his sister Margaret at the front displaying one of the placards. He photographed groups of gatherers, sorters and cleaners, and finally the enormous pile of sacks of sphagnum Moss collected on the pier ready to be shipped south.

Saving in the government's war schemes was considered patriotic, and Shetland responded with nineteen War Saving Associations. The islanders invested a disproportionately high amount, thought to be three times the national average. Novel approaches were taken to promote war savings. In the spring of 1918 a Tank Bank toured Shetland raising money from the sale of War Bonds and War

Saving Certificates. Charlie's photograph captures the life-size tank mounted on wheels, with two sailors and a relaxed pipe smoking lieutenant in charge, outside the Victoria Refreshment Rooms in Lerwick. Memorabilia included postcards and miniature tank money boxes.

Not everyone agreed with the government's schemes for raising money for the war and comments were made that this was a "Charity War" relying on freewill offerings from the public.

Lerwick mourned the death of Lieut. George Drewry VC accidentally killed on the 2nd August, 1918, while in command of HMT *William Jackson* on northern patrol. He had been awarded the VC on the 25th April, 1915, during the Gallipoli Campaign in the Dardanelles. He was the first merchant seaman to receive the VC. The coffin was borne on a gun carriage accompanied by fellow officers and followed by hundreds of mourners, servicemen and Shetlanders. Charlie's sister Margaret visited Lieut. Drewry's parents in London and described the funeral and the sadness felt throughout Shetland. Charlie had taken several photographs of the funeral cortege which Margaret gave to Mr and Mrs Drewry.

During the war the shop was a hub of information and gossip, and Charlie never missed an opportunity to record any interesting or unusual events. He was kept busy in the chemist shop, but still found time for sporting activities. The family were well known and highly regarded throughout the islands where he fished the burns and lochs for sea trout and salmon. Wherever he went there was always a welcome and a cup of tea, and he no doubt shared his catch with them. He was a good shot and supplemented the Medical Hall larder with game in season. Charlie rarely visited Noss during the war years, and I notice on one occasion he had written in the visitors' book "chemist" after his name, confirming that he was in a reserved occupation.

Relations with the admiralty were strained. Travel restrictions were a nuisance and in March 1916 permits became necessary for travel between islands in Shetland. This restriction was a great inconvenience. Doctors and ministers had to visit island communities and families were isolated. Under the Defence of the Realm Act, DORA the admiralty was in charge, in theory Shetland was under martial law! Charlie however, continued to visit Bressay and occasionally Noss, assisted no doubt, by his many naval friends.

Charlie's uncle, Thomas Mainland, was the headmaster of the Bressay School and the young Stout and Mainland cousins were good companions. His young cousin Harold took Charlie to see and photograph a large mine that had been washed ashore on a beach on Bressay. Was it still active?

Charlie photographed the territorials on parade, in camp and off duty. His brother James who had joined the Sea Forth Highlanders came home on leave before being sent to France. James was pleased as punch with his uniform, especially the kilt, and posed for a number of photographs. Cousins from Australia in their slouched hats, and kilted Canadians, who had enlisted, came to Shetland on leave and Charlie photographed them out and about with family and friends.

The ratings on the ships deployed from Busta Voe had a poor time in way of recreation. The officers went shooting and fishing and a service car went daily to Lerwick where they were welcomed into the social life of the town and joined their fellow officers who were stationed in Lerwick. The two youngest Stout girls, Queenie and Harriet were frequently photographed by Charlie in the company of naval officers. Swapping hats seems to have been all the rage!

August 1919 and the war is over. Charlie can now venture openly along the esplanade with his camera and notices young boys who have gathered on the landing steps to greet American sailors coming ashore from the USS *Panther*. The American ship was part of a flotilla of minesweepers clearing the North Sea of treacherous mines. The American sailors added to the already heady mix of people in Lerwick at the end of the war, and according to *The Shetland Times* "painted the town red!"

1919, the war was over in Europe but revolution had broken out in Russia. The camouflaged "dazzle" ship *Nairana* lying in Bressay Sound sailed to and from the White Sea in Russia evacuating white Russians and Cossacks adding yet more colour to the cosmopolitan population of Lerwick.

Photography soon became an important part of the business. Customers could buy cameras and film and have their photographs developed and printed in the shop. Charlie also had his own photographs on display for customers to see and order prints.

Charlie was everybody's pal. Generous to a fault, his nieces and nephews loved him. He was the uncle every child dreamed of. He kept open house for family and friends and helped many friends financially with their business proposals.

After the war the chemist shop continued to prosper and Charlie purchased a second chemist shop on the outskirts of town. He had a nose for business. I was astonished to see an advertisement in *The Shetland Times* for tulip bulbs imported from Holland courtesy of C.B. Stout.

He bought a movie camera and was usually among the first on the scene of any breaking news events. The Lindberghs arriving in Bressay Sound in their seaplane, the SS *Sunniva* on the rocks at the back of Mousa, the first airmail flight to Shetland etc. He had a motor boat, a motor car, a Shetland model sailing boat and presented a silver cup for the dipping lug race to the Lerwick Boating Club. He built a holiday house overlooking the beach at Sound and maintained a large house in Lerwick. He continued to make extended visits to his many friends in Holland and Norway, surprising his sisters once in Paris!

However did he find time to do any work?

Senior Naval Officer's Office
LERWICK......Jan. 20/1917.

PERMISSION is hereby granted to
Mr T Mainland of Bressay
to use a Camera, subject to the restrictions
laid down in Art. 19 of the Defence of the
Realm Regulations.
 Proofs of all photographs taken
are to be submitted to me
 This Permit is valid till...July 31/17

Commander, R.N.
SENIOR NAVAL OFFICER
and
COMPETENT NAVAL AUTHORITY.

Permit to take photographs during the war, 1917.

The *Oceanic* passing Bressay Lighthouse.

HMS *Implacable* with the two funnels, depot ship
for the five minesweeping naval trawlers.

The ship Z1 – the *Ice Whale*.

The ship Z5 – the *Pilot Whale*.

A convoy escort at anchor while the convoy gathers in Bressay Sound.

Submarine in Bressay Sound.

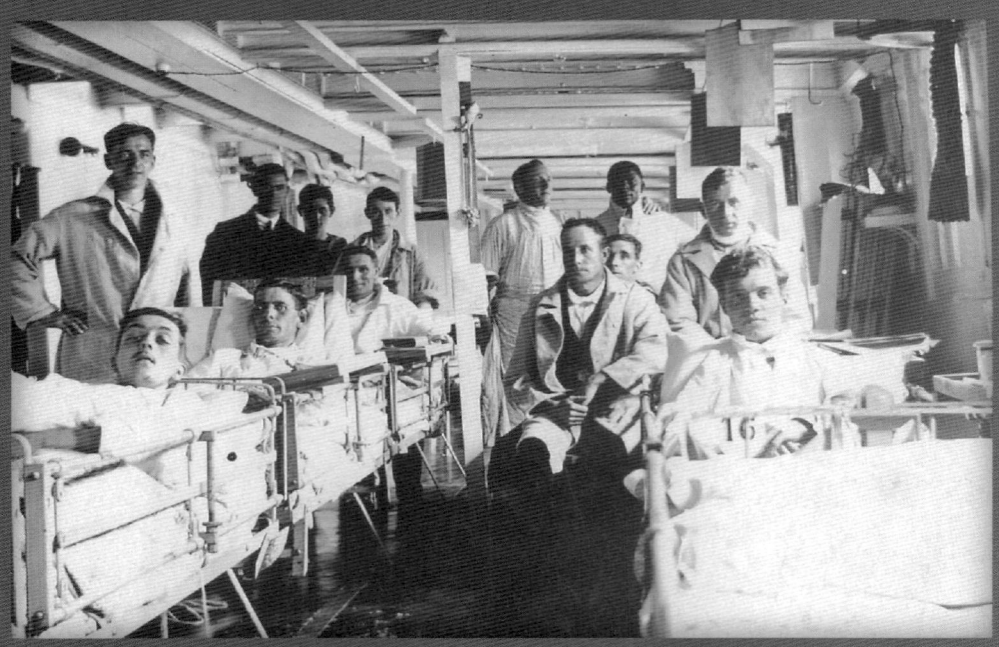

Sick and injured crewmen of the 10th Cruiser Squadron on board the hospital ship *Berbice* in Bressay Sound.

Observation balloon on Lerwick pier, 1914.

A convoy gathers in Bressay Sound.
Observers search the sea for submarines from the balloon.

The explosion at Alexandra Wharf Lerwick, April 1915.

Rear Admiral William Fawckner's car and driver.

The War Saving's Association "Tank" on a money raising tour.

The funeral of Lieut. George Drewry VC. The first merchant seaman to be awarded the Victoria Cross.

The gun carriage bearing the coffin of Lieut. George Drewry VC, 1918.

Lieut. George Drewry VC

Harold Mainland beside a mine washed ashore on Bressay.

Charlie and Roy visiting the Territorials in camp at Heogan.

Australian cousin in Shetland on leave from France.

The SS *Nairana* a "dazzle" (camouflaged) ship
seen from the drawing room windows.

American sailors coming ashore Lerwick.

The apprentice at the shop door. Photographs by Charlie on display.

Charles Lindbergh's Locheed Sirius seaplane in Lerwick harbour, August 1933. Anne Lindbergh is on the seaplane and Charles Lindbergh is climbing into the cockpit. The name of the seaplane, *Tingmissartoq* is native Canadian for "thought flies".

The *St Sunniva* wrecked on the rocks at Mousa, 1930.

Charles Lindbergh and his wife Anne arriving at the Bressay slipway at the Harbour Trust launch, surrounded by local dignitaries, August 1933.

Charlie on board *De Hoop* bound for Holland and new adventures.

Margaret in Shetland costume on her way to recite poems in dialect, written by her sister Betty, at a concert in Lerwick.

Margaret Bannatyne Stout 1894-1982
The Years Before the War

Margaret Bannatyne Stout was halfway through a three year course at the Edinburgh College of Domestic Science when the First World War broke out in 1914.

Following in the footsteps of her elder sisters, Margaret was an accomplished watercolour artist, won several national literary prizes for essays and verse, and was a founder member and leading light in the Pickwick Club, a dramatic society started by a group of girl friends at the Anderson Institute. Their first concert, which ended with a dramatisation of the Sleeping Beauty, is reported in full by *The Shetland News*. Margaret has caught the eye and ear of the reporter in this rave review.

> The difficult part of acting the wicked fairy fell to the lot of Miss Margaret Stout, when this little girl turned to the audience, and in the most intense and tragic tones, stated the calamity that would befall the Princess, when she reached the age of sixteen, the wicked fairy reached a stage in histrionic art scarcely conceivable in a girl of her years.

Margaret continued to receive rave reviews in *The Shetland News* after reciting a poem written in Shetland dialect by her sister Betty Stout.

> Miss Meg Stout has frequently performed before Lerwick audiences, and on every occasion has received quite an oration. She was dressed as an old Shetland wife. She received an enthusiastic encore and responded by giving "Loves Young Dream" by Haldane Burgess which drew forth loud laughter and applause.

Holidays could have been trying, with a house full of lively high spirited children, but Mrs Stout had the situation in hand, and children were dispatched to relatives in the country and to the mainland, leaving the Medical Hall for visiting friends and relations. Mrs Stouts sister Mary had married Joseph Strathern, headmaster of the school at Edderton on the Dornoch Firth, and Margaret and Francis spent happy and exciting holidays with their aunt and uncle and six cousins. Across the firth they could see Skibbo Castle, the home of Andrew Carnegie the millionaire philanthropist,[1] and every summer he gave a garden party for his neighbours. The highlight of the day was the children's race. Margaret recalls the excitement of the occasion.

> Andrew Carnegie stood in the porch of the Castle with a golden guinea in his hand. The race was for local children, much to our disappointment, so we stood with our Aunt and Uncle in the porch beside Andrew Carnegie who must have realised that we would have liked to join in the race, and told our Uncle to be sure we had a good tea. The winner was the first to reach Andrew Carnegie, who pressed the golden guinea into their hand. He was man of small stature and I often thought of that day when I entered the Andrew Carnegie library in Canterbury, one of the hundreds of libraries he founded across the country.

Other holidays were spent near Liverpool with a second cousin who was a sea captain. One of the excitements was a visit to Mark's Penny Bazaar, where everything cost one penny. The bazaar crammed with untold delights was magic to a child clutching her penny. This was the start of Marks and Spencer, and years and years later Margaret recalled the excitement of her visit as a child to Marks Penny Bazaar, to the chairman of M&S at a shareholders meeting. He was very proud of their humble beginnings and entrepreneurial spirit, and was amazed and delighted to meet someone who could remember the birth of M&S.

I think she was quite feisty. She stood her ground when headmaster Kirton dismissed her plan to study at the Edinburgh School of Cookery instead of classics at the University of Edinburgh.

---

1 Andrew Carnegie, Scottish born US industrialist and philanthropist, arriving in the United States as a penniless boy, he became one of the world's richest men and gave more than £70 million to charities, particularly education, in the United States and the United Kingdom.

Members of the Pickwick club in a dramatisation of "The Sleeping Beauty." From left. Flora Campbell, Margaret Stout, Rita Loggie, Patty Williamson, Margaret Anderson, Katherine Nicolson, Mary Campbell, and the young herald, Queenie Stout.

Shetland Sphagnum Moss Day, 9th August, 1917. Margaret at the front of the procession.

Margaret Bannatyne Stout 1894-1982

The War Years

1914. Margaret Stout was in her 2nd year at the Edinburgh School of Cookery, now Queen Margaret University. She writes in her diary.

One day I met a Lerwick boy who was at Edinburgh University, "I've just been gazetted" I enquired what that meant? He said he had got his MA degree, had been given a commission, and was now a lieutenant! That was the beginning. Soon all the fellows in our class and others had enlisted or been called up and half of them never came back. They got caught up in the battles of the Somme, Ypres and Albert.

I graduated from college with a first-class diploma and came home in 1915 to a strange bustling Lerwick. A destroyer base, navy everywhere. Mama was engrossed in war work. There was only one post for a domestic science teacher in Lerwick and that was filled. Before I had time to adjust, Mama announced that the headmaster of the school in Cullivoe, Yell, who was in the RNVR had been called up, and the school would have to close if a teacher could not be found. The Rev. McFadyen from Yell and a friend of Mama had an idea. Would I consider teaching there and keep the school open until a permanent teacher was appointed?

Nothing daunted I set off. I stayed with the McFadyens and he drove me to school in a pony and trap. I soon found lodgings with a family near the school, and quite enjoyed teaching in a village school. I gave the children two or three half holidays while I went fishing with my host's son!

Then a fellow student wrote and asked me to fill in for her for three months teaching Domestic Science at MacDuff High School in Scotland, which I did.

Margaret arrived in MacDuff and was immediately recruited to lead a Food Economy Campaign in MacDuff and District. She chaired public meetings, gave lectures and demonstrations, the main theme was to introduce simple nourishing ingredients and NO WASTE!

A Family at War

The local paper reported:

> A public meeting was held recently which was addressed by Miss Stout who explained the purpose of the campaign which was to give practical demonstrations in the school in war economy dishes. A committee of ladies has been formed to assist Miss Stout in a house to house visitation.

Quite brave really considering she had just graduated from college, but Margaret was never lacking in self confidence.

Margaret left MacDuff in July for home after waiting four days in Aberdeen for the boat. Margaret takes up the tale.

> Glorious weather – big party on board with all the students – like old times. The boat took four days to reach Shetland – we lay in Kirkwall two days – heavy firing at Scapa Flow - saw sea planes. Lerwick a destroyer base so very busy – reported as the second port in the world for shipping!!! War everywhere – casualty lists growing heavier and heavier. All our Australian cousins coming over.

On her return to Shetland Margaret continued the Food Economy Campaign. The War Savings Committee asked her to give a lecture and demonstration in Lerwick. "War Time Cookery" was reported in full in *The Shetland News*, one and a half columns!

Miss Stout explained that the enemy were intent on starving us into submission. Are we going to back up our men by playing our part? For food economy is the woman's part, and thus make victory secure? … before the war we imported 4/5th of our wheat … our food ships are being sunk daily, and it will go on, until we are able to combat submarine warfare … the Germans have been trying to force peace on us by starving us … it is a race against time … he who can endure the longest will win … by exercising the strictest economy in foodstuffs especially bread and sugar. Our very existence depends on it … the men fighting for us demand it … are their sacrifices to be in vain because we refuse to eat less? … to adults I would say…

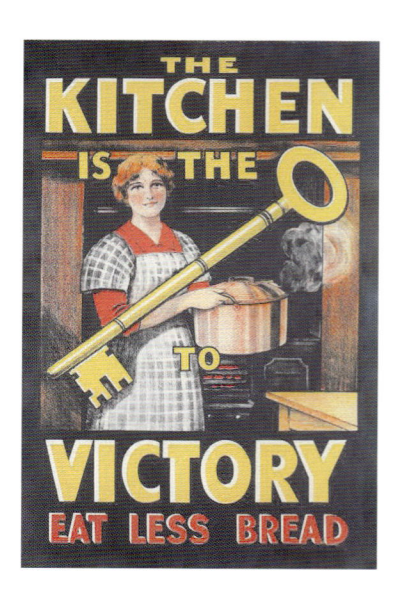

1. Eat one slice of bread less a day.

2. Save every crust or crumb of bread and utilise it in some way
3. Discourage the desire to eat between meals

It has been said that the kitchen cupboard is the civilian's trench and must be defended. Just in time we understand Germany's move to secure victory for herself but if we can tide over the next few months we shall win. (Loud applause.)

Miss Stout prepared and cooked various dishes.

The cheap and homely fresh herring stuffed with oatmeal and baked. The despised maize flour is hardly recognisable when mixed with ordinary flour in scones, and savoury pancakes. Flaked maize is used alone and undisguised in the form of fritters, a capital substitute for potatoes with meat!

The Shetland News reported her lecture in full, noting that Miss Stout had been sent by the school board in MacDuff to take part in a conference in Aberdeen, on war time cooking, so she was specially qualified for the work.

Margaret's lectures on war time economy did not go down too well in Shetland, comments were made that the Shetland diet was frugal enough! A letter to *The Shetland Times* in 1917 commented, "In a community like Shetland, and any such frugal people, it is useless to preach a gospel of economy".

Margaret was not daunted by these remarks and turned her attention to other areas of war economy. During the war sphagnum moss was collected by the public on a grand scale and used as an antiseptic dressing for wounds in army hospitals and on the battlefields. For centuries the antiseptic quality of moss had proved a valuable asset in times of conflict. Col. Cathart, senior surgeon at Edinburgh Royal Infirmary, approved the general use of moss, and suggested that people all over Britain could collect moss and dispatch it to collection centres. Sphagnum moss from Shetland was particularly desirable because of the presence of iodine from the salt spray.

In April 1917 Provost Goodlad received an urgent appeal for moss from the War Dressing's Store in Edinburgh. The town council declared 9th August to be "Shetland Sphagnum Moss Day" and a public holiday so that everyone from Skaw in Unst to Sumburgh Head could participate. Boat owners ferried people between islands and vehicle owners drove people to good spots to gather moss.

Margaret was beginning to be regarded, in spite of her food economy campaign, as a champion of woman's war work, and took a lead in the mass collection of sphagnum moss on 9th August, 1917. Charlie captured the moment before the principal working party set off in procession, Margaret at the head supporting one of the eye catching placards. The second placard suggests that refreshments will be available at the end of the day.

Charlie later photographed the mound of sacks of sphagnum moss on Victoria Pier awaiting shipment. By October 1917 an astonishing 2,437 sacks of moss had been shipped south from Shetland. Sphagnum moss continued to be collected until the end of the war and Margaret often joined groups of family and friends on moss collecting expeditions. Everyone wanted to take part. Charlie captured on film ladies in large hats sitting rigidly on the hillside accompanied by girls in sensible working clothes and aprons.

Margaret joined her mother and sisters at QMNG in the county hall to sew garments for war victims, and she was often asked to bake for fundraising teas and suppers. In July 1917 Margaret writes in her diary:

> Sphagnum moss and canteen work keep me busy. We have the cottage Noustigarth on Bressay with our own boat for the summer. Enjoy these lovely rows about the harbour on calm nights watching the convoys gather and leave.

Margaret really wanted to join the Woman's Royal Naval Service, the WRENS. and had been offered a commission but declined because she was so petite and thought that she would feel self conscious in uniform. Something she later regretted.

After receiving the news that James had been wounded at the Battle of Arras in April 1917, and was now receiving medical care in a London hospital, the family were anxious to have first hand news of him. Margaret volunteered to go to London, visit her brother, report back to Shetland, and then find war work.

> So off I went. Landed at Euston Station one morning in September and walked to the nearest hotel, the Euston, and asked at the reception desk for a room. The lady looked coldly at me and said, "We don't give rooms to SINGLE LADIES". I was dumbfounded. I asked to see the manageress and explained why I had come to London. She apologised and said of course I could stay, got a map and showed me Woolwich miles away. I set off by bus leaving my case in her care.

Margaret eventually arrived in Woolwich and found the hospital, the Brook, but James was out visiting a cousin, Laurence Sinclair from West Australia, who had enlisted, but had been drafted to oversee a munitions factory in Woolwich, and was living near the hospital. Margaret found the house and James and Lawrence who were so pleased to see her, she knew at once that her journey had been worthwhile. James was wearing the blue hospital clothes for wounded Tommies, and considering one leg was now two inches shorter, was remarkably cheerful and just longing to get home. He would always have to wear special handmade boots to compensate for the loss of two inches from one leg. The five shillings a week disability allowance from a grateful government, did not even cover the cost of his boots. But, he must have known how lucky he was, one of 57, to have survived the Battle of Arras.

Suddenly the sirens sounded and guns started firing, a Zeppelin was flying overhead. All the lights were extinguished and we flew to the front door and flung it open and stared up into the night sky. Far, far above us sailed a cigar shape of bright silver in the full glare of several search lights, our guns made a deafening roar and shells burst around her, but she was too high to be hit. The night was still, and the spectacle was unworldly. We watched the Zeppelin fly into cloud, and disappear and thought of the men onboard.

I experienced other Zeppelin raids on London. The siren went one day as I was running for a bus, of course everyone stopped and looked up at this gigantic cigar shaped balloon flying at great height. I put my hand in my pocket, purse gone! I blurted out my story to a policeman, "A pickpocket is doing very well here, thanks to that Zeppelin, you are the fourth person to report a stolen purse." He lent me a shilling which I returned in stamps.

My money was running out, so I applied for war work and was asked to run a canteen for war workers in the city. I was recommended to a Young Woman's Christian Association (YWCA) guest house in Highbury and got a room there. It was clean and cheap and full of rules and regulations, but it was a fine old house. The other girls there were teachers and secretaries in government departments. I decided to stay on longer in London, applied to the London County Council for a position on their staff and was appointed to a Jewish School in Cable Street in the City.

Margaret continues her diary with news of life in wartime London.

The Y.W.C.A. was run by a very straight-laced lady, Mrs Hollyberry, who would never be tolerated today. She had a master switch in her room and sharp at 10.30 she switched off all the lights! We had to be in by 10 to stop us going to the theatre of which she did not approve. But we went! We arranged with another girl to hear our tap at the window and let us in.

Gemany's aerial bombing campaign against Britain with London as the prime target, put civilians in the front line for the first time.

Raids are very frequent now, Mrs H insists on us turning out of bed and coming down to the basement. We finally persuaded her to let us stay in the drawing room, some of the girls very nervous but it doesn't seem to bother me. Hate this hymn singing to drown the sound of guns, very loud when the gun in the nearby field begins to fire. We hung out of the drawing room window one night to see the flashes from the guns in Highbury Fields and Mrs H came up and caught us.

December 18th – James leaving for home and his desk at the Commercial Bank. I was to go to the station to see him off, but the siren went, a raid. Worried as to his whereabouts, finally he turned up in Highbury while I was hunting for shrapnel out in the road. Trains all delayed, doubt he will miss the boat. Still the raids go on, getting quite used to them now. Bomb dropped on Highbury Fields but entered soft ground and did not explode or we should all have been blown up! I never go to bed without warm clothes to put on in case of a sudden call.

I was now doing two voluntary war jobs as well as teaching. Another teacher and I organised the early morning shift at the Red Cross Hut on King's Cross Station. We left Highbury at 6.30am without even a cup of tea. The train from Scotland arrived at the station at 7.30 and we had to be ready to serve a good breakfast to the soldiers returning to France. I enjoyed meeting the Scottish boys, occasionally Shetlanders, all in good spirits. By 8.30 we were glad to sit down and have a cup of tea. Then back to Highbury and on to school.

The other job I did was with another girl from Highbury, a Minister's daughter, at the Young Men's Christian Association (YMCA) recreation hut at Waterloo Station, it was a place for servicemen who had nowhere to go, perhaps waiting for a train. We arrived about 5.30 and closed about 10pm. We made refreshments and played games and had a sing song. I still have my autograph book from that time, you can see a page or two now. I settle the question of homesickness on Christmas Day and New Year's Eve by helping others. Since I couldn't be at home I might as well be on duty at the Hut and help the boys away from home. We had a great time and I thoroughly enjoyed it. I often wonder what happened to Francois Bieraimie decorated by Marshal Foch, Douglas Goudie, Canada, Samuel MacMillen, Royal Air Force, and all the others.

In December Margaret received a letter from Lieut. Hutchison whom she had met at the Recreation Hut, hoping to see her on his leave in April. Sadly, on the 17th April, 1918, she receives a letter from his mother to say that he has been killed in action, and will not be coming back on leave as expected. Margaret comments sadly, "like so many others".

Margaret had a succession of visitors at Highbury, many were naval personnel who had received hospitality in the Medical Hall. She led a busy social life thanks to the Shetland connection.

Lieut. Frank Johnson RNVR "Johns" who was living in the Grand Hotel across the street from the Medical Hall, had become a family friend. His home was in Richmond and when he was on leave we explored old London together. Johns knew I had studied Chaucer at school and took me to see the Inn at Southwark where the pilgrims gathered before setting off for Canterbury. He was an authority on old

London and had written books on the subject and our friendship continued when I married and moved to Kent.

Captain Christcesco from the SS *Juil*, turns up again, impressing the other girls at Highbury with his gold braid and sonorous voice. He sent a bellboy with a luncheon invitation, and to accompany him in the afternoon on a tour of London's bridges. Back at the hotel after dinner, I thought he was becoming a little too familiar, so I made my excuses, work next day, and left for Highbury. I wonder if he was ever united with his family in Rumania? We did meet some strange people during the war.

Capt. Smith RN had Shetland roots and felt quite entitled to make the Medical Hall his social base in Lerwick. He insisted that we, in return, visit him in Southampton. It was my turn and I set off rather nervously. We walked to his house from the railway station, and all the time he conversed in a LOUD voice telling me of all the captains who lived in the large houses we passed. One would have thought he was on the bridge of his ship. I was most embarrassed. But he entertained me like royalty and I had a wonderful weekend.

Captain W.E. Smith DSO RD RNVR had a distinguished war record. He was Captain of HMS *President* 1915, Commander HMS *Duke of Cornwall* 1916, Commander HMS *Roseabell* 1917, and Commodore of Convoy 1918. His loud voice was probably an asset.

Our cousin Jack Sinclair from Perth, West Australia, had enlisted and arrived in London on leave from France, now Lance Corporal Jack Sinclair of the Australian Imperial Forces. He looked me up in London and took me to the theatre. 'Maid of the Mountain', 'Chou Chin Chow', etc. He was a jolly fellow and I liked him awfully. So chummy right away. The Australian army pay was much higher than the Tommie's so they had money to spend on taxis, stalls in the theatre, and supper afterwards. I had two weeks holiday so he came to Shetland with me to meet the family.

Betty also came home on leave at the same time from France in her Croix Rouge uniform and Charlie captured the reunion on film. Margaret writes in her diary "Everybody in love with Jack, even myself getting enamoured".

11th November, 1918. The Armistice.
Margaret was in London and wrote this letter home which was published in *The Shetland News*.

What a day! We closed the school! Everyone went to Trafalgar Square! London went mad! I am just dying to know how the great good news about the armistice was received at home. It has been great here ever since. I wouldn't have missed being in London at this particular time not for anything! We got the news so quickly too. I may say that all London went absolutely mad at first over the news. People simply didn't know what they were doing or even cared. The officers seemed to lose their heads more than the men.

Of course everybody rushed out into the streets and thronged the busier quarters such as the Strand, Trafalgar Square and Piccadilly. In the afternoon and evening these places were a seething mass of people. They boarded taxis, busses, government lorries, RAF cars and commandeered any kind of vehicle even carts. The busses were like moving grandstands, people were jumping on and off without paying. Fancy people sitting on the outside of busses, the part over the driver's head, with their feet dangling down, or waltzing up and down the passages on top! On the top of a drivers cab on one bus, an officer, a private, a WREN and a WACC were dancing.

They were waltzing up and down Regent Street and a double set of lancers was going on outside Highbury Station, soldiers and girls. A Staff Officer and a RAF girl sitting hugging each other from sheer joy on the top of a taxi before thousands of people in Trafalgar Square. I saw as many as 20 people on a taxi intended for only 4, mostly standing on top waving flags and shouting themselves hoarse cheering.

Anybody could jump on anything. I saw wounded Tommies and munition girls being hauled up the steep sides of government cars which were already packed full to over flowing. What looked most idiotic of all, though, was soldiers and officers wearing girls hats with flags tied round them. The flappers from the Air Board offices rushed out onto the balconies and strewed the streets with plans of aeroplanes nipped into little bits, and emptied waste paper baskets galore, while the typists from the basements, rushed into the streets and banged the tin cases of their typewriters like drums.

The restaurants at night were thronged with the same festive crowd. An admiral was seen careering around with a saucepan on his head! It was nice though to see the happy look on the soldiers faces.

A girl who works in the admiralty told us her experiences. As soon as the news came they all rushed round to Downing Street, and the crowd yelled in unison, "come out Lloyd George", and at last he did appear and addressed the people. "I'm glad to tell you that the war will be over at 11 o'clock today." The housemaids waved their mops and feather dusters from upstairs windows. The two admiralty girls had then gone round to the back door, where they found him shaking hands with people, so they touched him! Most comical.

We all rushed to Buckingham Palace and roared, "We want King George", and after a little while he came out on the balcony and everybody cheered and shouted and sang God Save the King. Flags were immediately thrust out of every window.

Great masses of people took a quieter turn of rejoicing and sought sanctuary in the great churches to offer thanksgiving and prayer. There was a special service in Saint Pauls' yesterday afternoon which the King and Queen and Princess Mary attended along with other Royals and great personages. We saw them pass through Trafalgar Square in an open carriage. They look just like their portraits except that the King seems smaller. I saw an officer halfway up a lamp post with a camera. He must have got a good snap as he was so near. From Trafalgar Square we went by way of the Mall to Buckingham Palace. All along the Mall were numbers of captured German guns. The crowd was already collecting for the return of the King and Queen, but we got a good position on the edge of the pavement, and didn't have very long to wait before they came along. All the crowd hung around the palace and in a little while the Royal Trio came out on the balcony and everyone cheered and sang God Save the King again! The King bowed and they all went in. Queen Mary waved a little flag she was holding in her hand on the end of a stick, round and round in a sort of dignified fashion, very amusing.

You know that lovely marble statue of Queen Victoria outside Buckingham Palace? Well, I noticed it was all scratched with people's feet. I noticed the day before three people were sitting in Queen Victoria's arms! I don't know how on earth they ever got up as the statue is ever so high. Today their Majesties are touring the East End where they haven't been for years.

Enough the score of royalty. I begin to feel like Mrs Gossip of Sketch fame! I don't think there will be so much excitement when the actual peace comes, as we know it's coming. The Armistice was like a thunderbolt.

The next excitement was the arrival of the invitations to Queen Mary's Garden Party at Buckingham Palace on 25th July, 1919. Harriet was staying at the YWCA with Margaret, and Anne was spending a few days with them en route to Cologne. The three girls were to represent Shetland's outstanding contribution to Queen Mary's Needlework Guild. What to wear? Anne had a very becoming Scottish Church's uniform. Margaret had noticed a shop near her school which was selling their stock of tropical clothing at reduced prices. She and Harriet each bought a beautiful cream tussor suit, perfect for the occasion, as you can see from the studio photograph they had taken on that special day.

Margaret describes their visit to the garden party at Buckingham Palace:

We went to town by bus, then hailed a taxi and said "Buckingham Palace!" We entered the palace through a side door, walked straight through and out to the gardens at the back of the palace which are lovely. Although the number of guests was large they occupied but a small portion of the extensive palace grounds, part of which is quite wild and rustic.

The guests made lines of travel, Queen Mary walked down these accompanied by a lady in waiting, bowing to the right and left, before she got to the end of the line, we hurried off and joined another line and got another bow. The Queen looked very dignified. King George was doing the same in another place, so we joined up there and saw him very close.

When we arrived we were given a ticket with the number of our tent for refreshments. The royal refreshment tent was a beautiful red and gold canopy supported by silver poles and open on all sides, but a cordon round it.

The Royal party took their refreshments standing, the table appointments were all of gold and the floral decorations here, and throughout the other tents, were pink carnations. We stood and watched the whole royal family having tea, just standing about! The Queen wore a silver brocaded hyacinth blue gown and a toque, the King and Princess were in khaki and Princess Mary in her VAD uniform. Two military bands were playing one at each end of the lawns. We went to our tent and I had delicious iced coffee and several dainty cakes!

After tea their Majesties walked informally among their guests. We had been told that Queen Mary had asked that the Shetland representatives be presented to her. We waited expectantly, the lady in waiting summoned us to the Queen who acknowledged us, and we curtsied. The Queen wished to thank the Shetland Branch for their outstanding contribution to her Guild and Anne replied on behalf of the Shetland Branch. The Queen moved on and we found ourselves in the company of the King again, Princess Louise, Prince Albert, and the Duke of Connaught. Princess Helena Victoria who was wearing YWCA uniform, saw that I was wearing the Red Triangle, and asked what work I had done for the YWCA. and seemed quite interested when I told her. But she was more interested to hear about war work in Shetland.

At 6.30 the Royal party returned to the Palace, when the National Anthem was again played. We made our way slowly out through the ground floor of the Palace, the walls of which were hung with well known paintings of Kings and Queens, the door of the white drawing room was open and we could see Princess Mary talking to a lady. Then up the grand staircase and out into the courtyard, through the gates, and our wonderful day was over.

It was now 1921, the war was over, and those that could, were picking up the threads of civilian life again. Margaret received an invitation from American friends to join them in Paris, where they planned to stay for some time. They thought that she would be a companion to their only daughter Mignon. Margaret was thrilled to be asked, and set off for Paris.

Margaret's American friends wanted to visit the battlefields where the American soldiers had fought, so they set off to explore the region from Reims to Verdun. They

Margaret Bannatyne Stout 1894-1982

took the train to Reims where a hired car and driver was waiting for them and set off on their travels.

Reims had been a frontline city throughout the war, captured by the Germans in 1914 for a few days and fought over continuously. The great cathedral, the medieval jewel of Europe was reduced to rubble. After the British victory at the battle of the Marne in 1914 the new front line was just a few miles north east of Reims and the cathedral was in range of German artillery now dug in at Vouziers. German officers told their gunners to avoid the cathedral, "off limits" to both sides, but changed their minds when they saw French artillery spotters directing fire onto German positions from the roof of the cathedral. Ordering immediate reprisal 200-300 German shells tore into the heart of the cathedral destroying, in minutes, centuries of religious fervour. After that, German shells rained down continuously on the cathedral and other historic buildings. Very few people stayed in the city as it became a battlefield for the remainder of the war.

> We walked on the streets between fragments of stone walls, fronts of buildings open to the sky, towards the great ruin that was the cathedral. We stepped cautiously over piles of rubble and stared at the jumble of splintered wood, chunks of carved stone arches and columns and fragments of glass glinting among the debris. I was unprepared for the vast scale of the destruction and could only gaze about me in disbelief. People spoke of the Martyrdom of Reims.
>
> The next day we set off for Fort la Pompelle through tracts of desolate country concealing miles of trenches pitted with shell holes, but already a soft green haze of grass covered the battlefields accentuating the blackened tree stumps. Creeping plants covered the barbed wire, bits of gun carriages and all manner of debris. In contrast to the ugly remains of war, areas of the ground were covered with great masses of red poppies and blue cornflowers, blooming defiantly. We were amazed at how quickly nature had taken over the abandoned battlefields. We passed through what had been a village, just heaps of stones, broken wood and the only recognisable ruin, the village church with its' shattered spire. We drew in and looked about, not a soul to be seen. The eerie silence was chilling.
>
> Near Fort Pompelle our driver stopped to show us a British tank which had been captured by the Germans, given a German identity with a Maltese Cross (the model for the iron cross) and used in battle against us. In 1918 a large number of British tanks had been captured at Fort la Pompelle. I poked around it and wish now that I had taken the Pickelhaube, pickle helmet, I found lying on the ground.

Margaret's American friends wanted to visit Chateau Thiery where in the spring of 1918 the American Expeditionary Force, in their first engagement, fought off a surprise attack by the Germans. The unexpected attack created an emergency and the AEF were rushed to the front. The 7th Machine Gun Battalion, despite being unprepared, succeeded in halting the Germans from crossing the Marne. This action became a decisive point in the war.

Margaret continues her tale.

> Our driver stopped to show us a curiosity. Lying on the ground was what appeared to be a large tree trunk with branches, covered with bark, but on closer inspection we realised that it was made from metal covered with real bark. A bogus tree. Inside was a short ladder and a spy hole near the top where an observer could scan the landscape unobserved to see what the enemy was up to.
>
> We drove on to Vienne le Chateau and visited Camp Moreau, a German Rest Camp hidden in a ravine, a beautiful place with small rustic log cabins, little stone houses and caves made from corrugated iron. The camp was well equipped with a hospital and underground galleries, the Germans had only vacated the camp in September 1918.

They continued through the Foret d'Argonne which in 1917 was the scene of the greatest battles and victory for the American Expeditionary Force. The American troops, new to war, held the ground for 47 days against seasoned German troops who had spent four years fortifying the rough hilly terrain. The battles raged two and fro until a final push by the Americans on 1st November when the enemy began

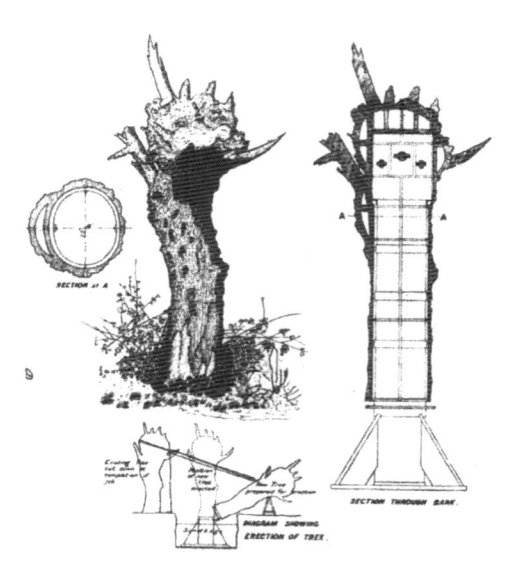

Royal Engineer design for bogus tree.   Bogus tree used as an observation post.

withdrawing across their entire front, exhausted. The Germans conceded defeat, and on 11th November the Armistice was signed. It was a baptism of fire for the Americans. 1.2 million American soldiers took part in the offensive and 26 thousand lost their lives.

> The Germans had constructed an impressive network of trenches, passageways and miles of galleries linked to the front line. We were shown some of the trenches and the debris of the last occupants, helmets, bits of clothing, boots, empty food tins, but the most interesting was the beautiful bunker belonging to the Kronprinz, son of Wilheim 2nd. Lined with wood, remains of furniture and a piano! I have a postcard showing the Kronprinz's elaborately built bunker in the forest.

They drove past Varrennes and on to Mount Falcon where the 39th U.S.A. Infantry Regiment fought and won their greatest battle in 1917 but not without cost. The Germans held the high ground, their artillery devastated the advancing infantry. The German commander was confident that he could hold out against these inexperienced Americans but underestimated the American resolve. After three days of heavy fighting, despite being ambushed in the forest, they took the heights of Mount Falcon. The American engineers had to repair the roads to enable supplies to keep up with the fast advancing troops. The Americans won the day but not without huge loss of life in both camps.

Their tour continued to Verdun where the bloodiest battles of the 20th century had been fought. Verdun was a fully modernised fortress which the Germans had refrained from attacking until February 1916. The massive attack drew in French reserves from every front, as the Germans intended. They planned to annihilate the French army leaving just the British army to defeat, but they had underestimated the French resolve. The massive and prolonged attack on the symbolic fortress of Verdun, was one of the bloodiest offences in military history. For five months the position held, but drained the life blood from the French army. Huge losses were sustained in both camps. 700,000 soldiers died or were wounded, nine villages disappeared, six never to be rebuilt.

Margaret describes the battlefields of Verdun.

> We stared at this grotesque landscape changed forever by the vast underground explosions perpetuated by both sides, forming lakes and mountains where none had existed before. No one is allowed to walk over this tortured landscape for fear of unexploded shells.
>
> Our guide was keen to show us a poignant memorial to the 137th French Infantry, the Trench des Baionnettes. On the 12th June, 1916, two battalions of

the 137th French Infantry who had been deployed at the front under appalling shelling, were cut off. The company had lost 94 out of 164 men, and the remaining poilus had been placed in a row of exposed trenches directly in view of German artillery spotters. The infantry were waiting in the front line trench with fixed bayonets to advance. When the German artillery ceased their bombardment, all that remained visible in the trench, were a number of bayonets protruding from the earth.

As a mark of respect, the Germans completed filling in the mass grave leaving the protruding bayonets marking each soldier's grave. When the war ended 40 bodies were exhumed and reburied in Fleuty Cemetery, the remaining 17 unknown were left where they lay, marked by simple wooden crosses, and of course, their bayonets.
Margaret writes:

> We were deeply moved by the story of the Trench des Baionnettes and to see and touch the bayonets was a strange link to those brave French soldiers. I have a picture of the trench and the bayonets among my war diaries.

A wealthy American moved by the story, commissioned a shelter with a canopy supported by cylindrical columns to cover and protect the graves and the bayonets for all time.

> Our guide told us many more moving stories. We stopped at Fort Vaux, one of the forts at Verdun, and he told us how the defence of this historic fort was marked by the heroism and endurance of the French garrison who repulsed the German assaults fighting hand to hand, the first large engagement inside a fort during the war. The last few soldiers surrendered on 7th June, 1916, after all support had ended, pigeons had been sent begging relief, the last communication sent by Major Raynal before they surrendered, read "This is my last pigeon." The German commander Crown Prince Wilhelm presented Major Raynal with a French officer's sword as a mark of respect. Fort Vaux was recaptured by the French and Americans in November 1916.
> On our return journey to Rheims we had lunch at the Hostel Cleric D'Argonne, before going on to visit the large German cemetery at D'Argonne and the Ossuaire at Douament, a grim place.
> My American friends decided that they would like to see something of the Western Front, so we drove from Reims to the British sector and visited Albert, Bapaume and Arras.
> On the road to Albert we saw signs of the battlefields, lines of trenches, dugouts

and shell holes, and remains of villages where here and there the inhabitants had returned to rebuild their homes from the ruins. The enterprising ones had souvenirs for sale to the increasing number of battlefield visitors. Some were living in wooden huts erected by the authorities on the edge of the villages.

Albert was the principal town behind the lines on the Somme battlefields. The town was devastated during the war and the population had fled. The road between Albert and Boiselle ran straight across the battlefields. We drew up in front of what had once been the pride of Albert, the great Cathedral now a gaunt shell. For three years every soldier who passed through Albert remembers the image of the Golden Madonna and Child toppled from the Cathedral Spire by enemy artillery in 1915, but left hanging from the Basilica. All sorts of predictions were made as to what would happen when the Madonna fell. Which she eventually did, brought to earth by shelling in 1918. We clambered over the broken stonework to see the shattered interior. I never realised the destruction was on such a vast scale, and that so many great churches and cathedrals were utterly destroyed in the war. And for what?

We continued through this wasteland and stopped to see the huge mine crater at La Boiselle. It was enormous and marked the start of the 1916 Somme Battle. Harry Lauder[1] came here to see the place where his only son was killed. He climbed into the crater and sang to the troops who had gathered around the perimeter the song he had written for his son. "Keep Right on to the End of the Road." It must have been very moving.

The next day they sped towards Arras, an ancient and beautiful town severely damaged by shell fire. They drove through ruined streets of once picturesque old houses and stopped in the Grand Place where they saw the ruins of the Hotel de Ville. Their guide showed them some of the ancient underground cellars and passages which our soldiers used to move supplies safely to the front line. The great cathedral, like all the others they had seen, stood roofless, the interior a jumble of great stone arches and pillars.

Beyond Arras at Fampaux we saw the landscape where my brother James went "over the top" in April 1917. The Highlanders walked into devastating German machine gun fire and were wiped out. James survived although he was twice wounded and eventually picked up by stretcher bearers and taken to a casualty station. I looked at the quiet green landscape and tried to imagine the scene as 375 Seaforth Highlanders advanced over the snow covered plain towards the German

---

1   Sir Harry Lauder was a popular Scottish songwriter and singer, a favourite with Kings and commoners.

guns. As the bullets found their mark the Highlanders pitched forward into the snow and the ranks closed in.

The Bapaume Post Military Cemetery is situated on the eastern outskirts of Albert, near Boiselle. The cemetery was consecrated in 1916 and 150 graves date from that time with the addition of another 250 graves after the Armistice. There is a photograph of Margaret and Mignon in the cemetery kneeling either side of a memorial to a Canadian Battalion.

THE OFFICERS N.C.O's & MEN
of the
14TH CANADIAN BATTALION
ROYAL MONTREAL REGt
Who Fell in Action
Near This Spot
1916

While researching First World War material, I was astonished to find a photograph of a Canadian soldier looking at the same memorial in 1916 when it had just been consecrated. I was interested to learn that the brass plaque on the memorial cross now hangs in the Royal Montreal Regimental Mess in Westmount, Quebec.

Margaret had been searching for the grave of her Australian cousin Private Henry Mainland who had been killed in action at Ypres in 1917. The family were deeply grieved that he had not had leave to visit the family in Shetland. Margaret was particularly sad because she had often written to his father on Sunday afternoons, with news from Shetland. The family owned a prosperous pearl fishing station in Australia and had gifted Margaret a beautiful gold and pearl pendant which she treasured.

In 2019 Graham Johnston, a Shetland friend, who is a researcher and writer on the First World War, visited the New British Cemetery, Dochy Farm, Belgium and found and photographed the war grave of Pte. Henry Owen Mainland. I am glad that my mother's quest has been resolved but sad that she is not here to bear witness.

Margaret's friends returned to America and she continued her travels to Holland where she met her brother Charlie. They stayed with their friend Dr Van Asperen and his family. She eventually returned to Shetland and completed *Cookery for Northern Wives*, published in 1922, the first Shetland cookery book.

Her sister Betty, married to an American naval officer in Paris, was sailing to America and a new life. Margaret went too.

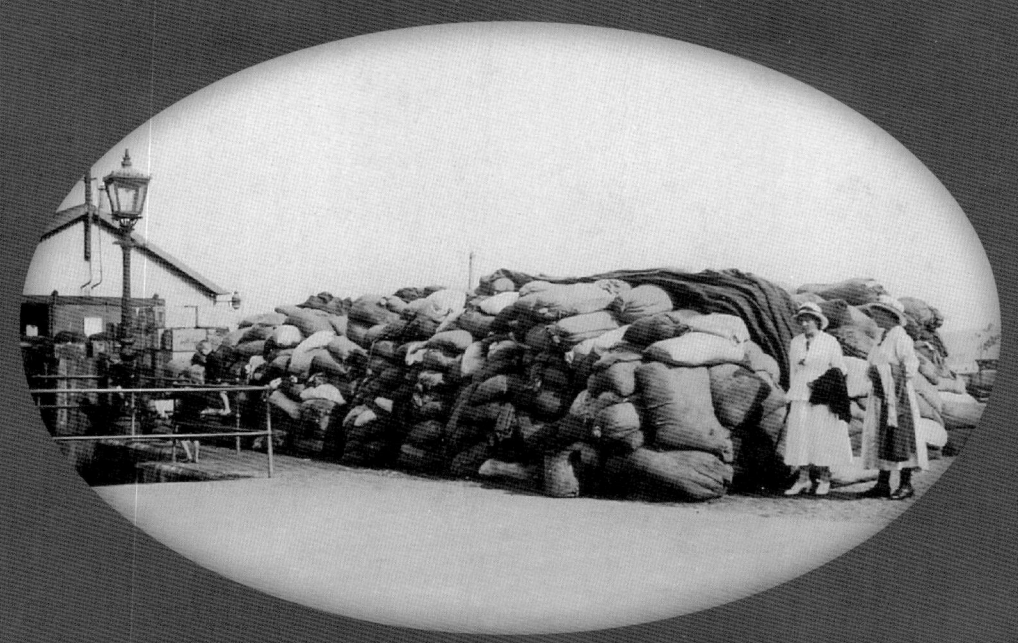

Sacks of sphagnum moss on Victoria Pier awaiting shipment south.

Margaret with Australian cousin on leave in Shetland.

New Year's Eve. 1918-19

Douglas M. Goudie.
ex Cadet in R.A.F.
Transferred from 29th Bn. Canadians.
Wounded Ypres 20th May 1915
Future address Kamloops
B.C.
Canada.

Christmas Night 1918
William Gait.
H.M. Minesweeper Newbury
Ireland,
By Bixton,
Shetland Isles.

Waterloo Annex
Social Room
Y.M.C.A.

Margaret in London wearing her YMCA wartime uniform.

I Wish I Where that
China Cup From Wish
You Sip Your tea and
Every Sip From that Cup
Would Mean a Kiss for Me

Yours
Samuel MacMillan
Royal. Air. Force

11 Oct 1918
Croix de Guerre

at Arras
Nov 18.
Decorated by Marshal Foch.
(real name François Bienaimie)

Three pages from Margaret's autograph book dating from her wartime work with the YWCA at the Recreation Hut, Waterloo Station.

11th November, 1918, Armistice Day, London. A London bus crowded with revellers.
Topical Press Agency

11th November, 1918. Armistice day. Trafalgar Square, London.
R.P.S. Science & Society

4.

> The Lord Chamberlain is commanded by Their Majesties to invite The Misses Annie, Margaret & Harriet Stout, Members of G.M.N. Guild (Shetland Branch) to an Afternoon Party in the Garden of Buckingham Palace on Friday the 25th July, 1919 from 4 to 6.30 p.m. (Weather Permitting)
>
> Morning Dress or Service Dress Uniform.

Invitation to Queen Mary's Garden Party at Buckingham Palace 25th July, 1919.

Studio photograph of Harriet, Anne and Margaret dressed for the Buckingham Palace Garden Party.

Margaret and Mignon outside a damaged Sacre Coeur Paris.

Margaret and Mignon in the ruins of Reims Cathedral.

Margaret and her American friends with a British tank, captured by the Germans and used in battle against us.

The well constructed shelter built for
the Kronzprinz in the Argonne.

Ossuaire de Douament.

Trauchee des Baionnettes.

The ruined Cathedral at Albert before the golden Virgin was toppled by artillery gun fire, 1918.

Cordoned off Hotel de Ville France.

Margaret and Mignon in the grounds of a ruined chateaux in France.

Margaret and Mignon in the ruins of Albert Cathedral in Northern France.

Margaret and Mignon kneeling beside a memorial to the
Canadian 14th Battalion, Royal Montreal Regiment, 1921.

A Canadian soldier standing beside the same memorial in 1916.
Library and Archives Canada

Margaret wearing the gold and pearl pendant given to her by Uncle Henry Mainland who owned a prosperous pearl fishery in Australia.

Cookery for Northern Wives by Margaret Bannatyne Stout. Reprinted by the Shetland Amenity Trust.

James in his Boy Scout uniform.

Roy, James and a friend.

James Stout 1898-1953
The Years Before the War

In 1912 the Scout movement was established in Shetland. The whole ethos of Scouting appealed to James who joined the first troop based in Lerwick. Charlie photographed his younger brother proudly wearing his Scout uniform, a foretaste of things to come.

James had just joined the Commercial Bank in Lerwick when war was declared. Banking was considered a suitable career for the second son.

He was 16 and yearned to be a sports master.

James was huge fun. A real prankster. His tricks on visitors were legendary. The skeleton from Dr Loeterbagh's day turned up regularly in visitors' beds, false faces from the guising trunk "gluffed" the long suffering maids who fortunately took it all in good part, though goodness knows what they told their families! The subdued gas and lamp light must have helped!

He clowns his way through endless picnics and family outings caught forever on camera by his brother Charlie.

Overshadowed by his dare-devil brother, the First World War gave James the opportunity to escape the humdrum atmosphere of the bank and to prove himself.

James in uniform wearing the tartan trousers of the
Seaforth Highlanders. Roy does not approve.

James Stout 1898-1953
The War Years

On 18th February, 1916, the day before his 18th birthday, James Stout persuaded the Commercial Bank to sanction his recruitment. He hurried to the recruitment office in Fort Charlotte where his name was the last entered under the "Derby Scheme". The scheme was initiated by Lord Derby, following the realisation that the number of volunteers was dwindling. The scheme required men aged 18 to 24 to attest their willingness to serve. Men who would not volunteer were labelled "shirkers". James was given an armband to wear as proof that he had enlisted thus avoiding the taunts and "white feather" treatment. Charlie photographed James proudly displaying the armband.

He left Shetland in March 1916 to join the Seaforth Highlanders for training in Dunfermline. On 15th September Karl Manson, a school friend and fellow recruit, wrote "I am in the same tent as James Stout, but as he is underage he will not go to Cromarty yet for training".

James and Karl returned to Shetland on 10 days leave at the end of September. Charlie photographed James in the uniform of the Seaforth Highlanders, showing off the kilt he had always longed to wear. The notes in the margins of the Medical Hall visitors' book record James home on leave September 1916.

March 1917, and James is posted to France. He writes "our small draft was posted to the 1/5 battalion and I was rejoicing that I would be with Karl again, but the next day we were told that we were for the 2nd Seaforth. *The Shetland News* reported on the "recent inspection of the 10th Seaforth Highlanders by Lord French, among the prize winners were Private James Stout and Private Karl Manson both of Lerwick."

Karl writing of James thought that "he was like all true sons of the "old rock" very anxious to hear any news of Shetland then so far away from us but always in our minds."

The 9th April marked the start of the battle of Arras. From 9th to 11th April James was "up the line". In General Sir Edmond Allenby's opinion the 11th of April was the "crucial day".

On the 11th April, 1917, the 2nd battalion of the Seaforth Highlanders in conjunction with the 1st battalion Royal Fusiliers, were ordered to launch an attack on the chemical works at Roeux. The orders had been meticulously written in longhand by Brigade Major Captain Hedworth Fellows MC. "At 10am Seaforths will advance in fours down road to crossroads, then up Sunken Road to Hyderabad Redoubt in position by 11am". But Fellows had not realised that Sunken Road was not "sunken" for the last 50 yards! And the Seaforths would be easily seen by the enemy in the chemical works.

A photograph taken by the Royal Flying Corps a few hours before the start of the battle indicated that the chemical works were completely intact and undamaged by the recent artillery barrage, and were strongly defended by machine guns. The Seaforths marched as ordered into Fampoux followed by the 1st Royal Irish Fusiliers, but were spotted by a German plane which swooped low over the marching column of men. Troops watching from houses in the village were amazed at this parade and shouted warnings to the Seaforth officers, that if they continued along Sunken Road they would be seen by the enemy, but they were ignored.

By 11am the Seaforths had crossed to Sunken Road and promptly come under machine gun fire from the chemical works. The Sunken Road was now becoming very congested and alarming as enemy shells fell among them. The Seaforths pushed their way along Huddle Trench and waited for zero hour. No military minds had seen the chemical works or surveyed the open ground devoid of cover which the Seaforths were expected to cross.

At 11.57am came the order to "fix baynets" and the Seaforths scrambled, swearing and slipping in the snow, up the side of the trench and out into the open, where the German machine guns had a perfect view of the thin line of highlanders advancing across the white plain towards them.

The weak barrage put down had been useless. No shells had fallen on the chemical works 1,500 yards ahead. The concentrated fire from 30 German machine guns was directed at the meagre line of celts. As the bullets found their mark, and men pitched forth into the snow, so the ranks closed in.

One second lieutenant of the Seaforths, badly wounded, wrote: "Right from the start it was a dreadful affair. A fine battalion totally destroyed. It was a total disgrace that the powers that be could order such an attack in full daylight and against such defences. We had no chance at all, and I lost many good friends."[1] Still exceedingly bitter at the memory of such a terrible day he did not want his name known.

The failure of Gosling's 10th infantry attack resulted in the collapse of the whole 4th division attack. General Lambton was furious, in spite of the fact that the 10th Brigade had lost 1,000 men out of 1,600 who had gone into the attack, he ordered them to attack again immediately! Gosling, receiving these orders at HQ one mile behind the action, and unaware that his own brigade no longer existed, ordered the nearest field artillery to bombard the chemical works, and the Seaforths to attack again. But there were no Seaforths left to carry out the attack.

---

1   Quote from a Seaforth second lieutenant who did not want his name given.

The unknown strength and positioning of the enemy's machine guns were responsible for the rout. The total losses sustained by the Seaforth Highlanders were all 12 officers, and 363 other ranks out of a total of 420 other ranks. 57 survived including the wounded.

"Many gallant acts were recorded during the great war, but there were few as courageous as the now forgotten advance of the Second Seaforth Highlanders on the 11th April 1917 at the battle of Arras."[2]

James Stout was very lucky to have survived. It is telling to read James' own account of the battle in a letter home, which was published in *The Shetland News* on 4th May, 1917. He had been wounded and was writing from Brook End Hospital, Woolwich. Let him tell you in his own words.

> I am now going to tell you a little of my news from France since we left the small village of ----. We left on the morning of the 9th and marched for miles, passing many a battery of artillery who were all going ahead pouring shells by the hundred at the Huns. We knew by this time that the "Big Push" had started.
>
> At last we came to a halt and settled down just off the road for a rest. We rested there for a few hours and had some dinner, and also got picks and shovels issued out and material for wiring. It was when we halted here that we saw first signs of the great battle, in the shape of the walking wounded cases. There were some really pitiable sights among them, but all seemed more or less glad to be out of it. One poor "kiltie" was coming down the road all covered in blood and mud, uniform in rags, and was being supported on both sides by Germans, big bulky looking brutes, but who were taking great care in helping this "jock" along. All those who were questioned as to how it was going said "Oh fine" and the Huns were being pushed back at a great rate. Next we saw batches of prisoners. Lots of 50 and 100 came past about every quarter of an hour, all seeming happy and smiling quite glad to be captured.
>
> We journeyed on from there past what had been our front line trenches, across "No Man's Land" and enemy lines of trenches. What an upheaval had been made by our artillery! Almost every yard of ground had been torn up by our shell fire. We had to proceed by platoons in single file to get across it. This place was still in range of the enemy's guns and occasionally one would burst about us. At last we got to the line of trenches where we were to spend the night, and at once started to make suitable dugouts for protection from shells etc.
>
> The ground was fairly sandy so we made quite nice little dugouts. At night we had a brilliant display of star shells and had a few "whizz bangs" knocking around but nothing to mention. We lived there for two nights, and found it pretty cold with the snow and

---

2   "Cheerful Sacrifice" by Jonathon Nicholls. Battle of Arras, 1917.

no great coat, only a waterproof sheet. We moved off next morning (11th) and passed through a village which had been used quite recently by the Germans but is in ruins now. We were then told that our barrage was starting at noon, so we knew when we'd begin. The road we were on was called "Sunken Road", and as we went forward, the height of the bank protecting us on our right got less and less, so that by the time we had got to the top we had only a foot or two to crouch down behind. We had to advance in small rushes, or on our hands and knees, the enemy machine guns spitting just above our heads. When we had got our proper distances we waited until the barrage started: and then we went over.

When our barrage began the enemy machine gun fire was about trebled and I wonder how our fellows managed to get through it, because the bullets seemed to be going over and about my head by the hundred. I kept my steel helmet well down over my face and my head down, rifle with bayonet slung over my right shoulder and my spade in my left hand as a protection for my throat.

I had gone about 300 yards when something struck me on top of the head and I fell flat. I was stunned for about 10 minutes, and when I put my hand up expecting to find a gash in my head, lo and behold there was nothing but a small lump about the size of a shilling. I ventured to take off my helmet because the bullets seemed to be flying at a higher range and found that a bullet had penetrated my helmet and followed the curve of the crown inside, and found a way out over my back or shoulder. It gave me a bit of a shock at first to think of the narrow shave I'd had. By this time our chaps were a good bit ahead, so I got up to go on the way again, but only got 50 yards or so when down I went again with a bullet through the right knee. That settled it that time, no more going on for me. I began to think what was the best way to get back, but found I couldn't crawl because the bone was broken. I managed to get part of my iodine and field dressing on, and then, with the help of my shovel, placed the right foot and leg on top of the left, and with entrenching tool handle as a splint, wound my puttees round both my legs, binding them together. When I had fixed that I found I could with difficulty crawl a little by lying on my back reaching back my hands and pulling back my legs after me. I had barely got a hundred yards when I had to give it up as hopeless.

I came across another fellow who was wounded, lying on his face. In the afternoon the snow began to fall, so I put my waterproof over me and lay patiently waiting for stretcher bearers to come. They came once or twice and took some cases further down the field. We lay and lay, and still the snow came down, but no signs of anybody. When night drew on and lights and flares went up, I thought that we had been forgotten about altogether, but at last they did come about 12.30 at night, and I was taken to 1st dressing station in the village we had passed through. The first thing I got was a cup of hot Horlick's malted milk, which I did enjoy, seeing that the only thing I'd had that day was a few small biscuits in the early morning. From there I travelled by motor ambulance and trains until I landed at 13th General Hospital Boulogne, crossed the Channel and landed at the Brook Hospital on Sunday night (15th) so that about ends my tale. I still have my souvenir helmet, have carted it about with me everywhere I went, so I wouldn't like to lose it now. Have to stop now as this is a beastly awkward position I'm writing in, lying on my back!

James wrote later:

After we left our billets for "up line" on the morning of the 9th Karl was often in my mind because I knew that the 51st Division was to "go over" that morning. When I was wounded on the 11th I had many a thought about Karl but never dreamed the worst had happened.

James must have been reported missing because a parcel sent to him from the Medical Hall had been returned. Charlie and the girls decided to say nothing to their parents until confirmation of James' fate. One can imagine their joy and relief on hearing that James was in hospital in Woolwich with a knee wound.

He underwent surgery at the Brook Hospital which left him with one leg two inches shorter than the other, and the prospect of wearing special handmade boots for the rest of his life.

James was in hospital for eight months and the photographs show James wearing the blue clothes for wounded Tommies, during his convalescence. The family in Shetland were anxious for firsthand news of James. Margaret volunteered to make the journey to London, visit James and find war work.

She arrived at the Brook to find James out visiting a cousin from West Australia who was an overseer in a munitions factory in Woolwich, and living near the hospital. They had a great reunion which was interrupted by a Zeppelin raid!

By mid December James was fit to travel home to Shetland and the bank. The joyful entry in the Medical Hall visitors' book on 28th December 1917, reads, "James returned. Killed the fatted calf!"

In the spring James visited Noss and wrote in the visitors' book 21st April, 1918. "1st visit for about "umpteen" years – spent best day for ages." The photograph of him clowning around on the beach with an old fishing float for a telescope and sheep's wool beard, reveals the built up boot which he had to wear as a result of his war wound.

The helmet with the bullet hole which had saved James' life was taken safely home and hung at the side of the drawing room fireplace in the Medical Hall. He remained remarkably cheerful, married a lovely lady called Nancy, and together they made their home in Dunfermline. The helmet of course, went with him.

James wearing his armband, evidence that he had enlisted.

James home on his first leave in the uniform of the Seaforth Highlanders.

James and his cousin James Smith from the Westing in Unst.

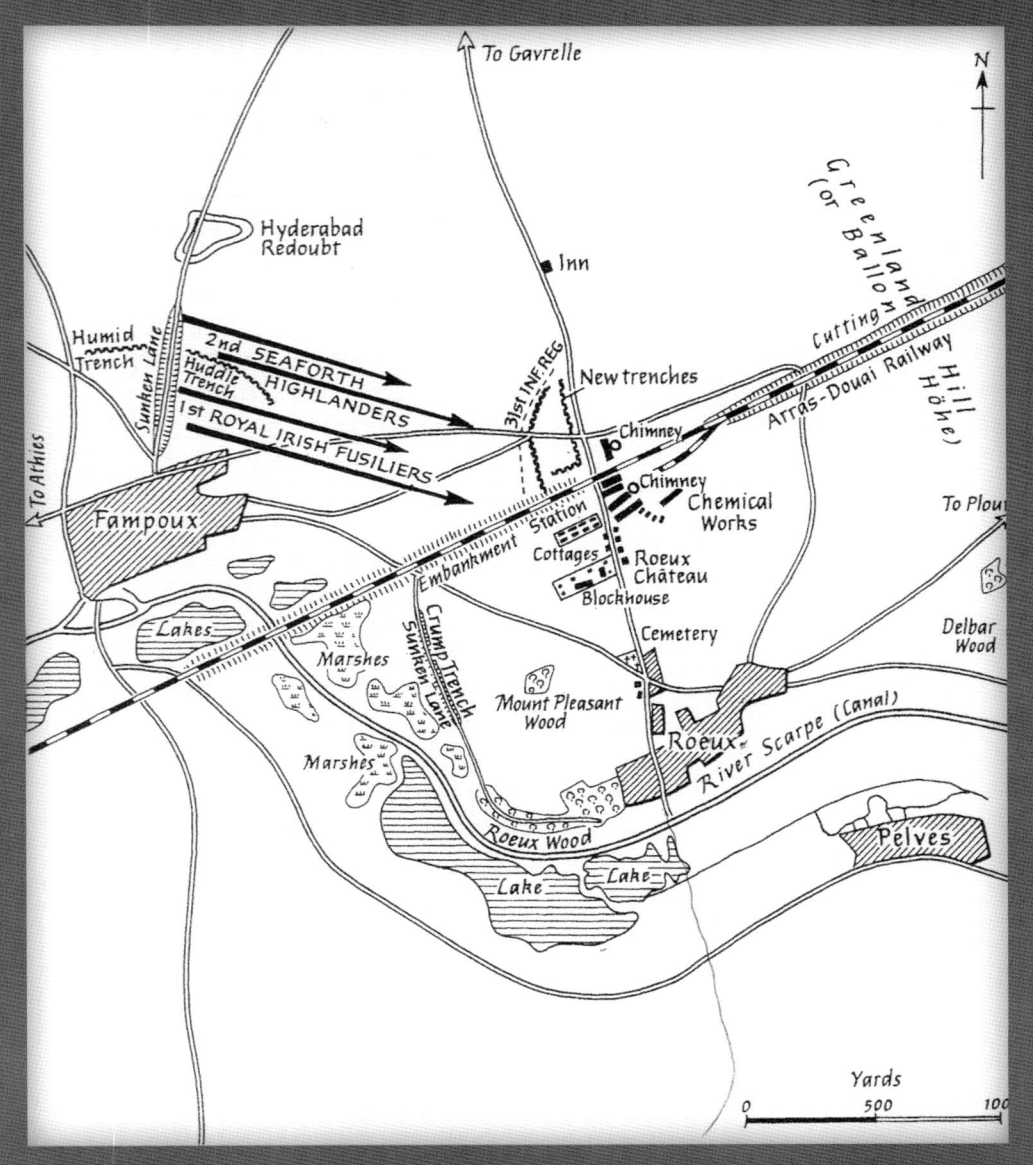

The route of attack by the 2nd Seaforth Highlanders towards the Chemical Works on 11th April 1917. "Cheerful Sacrifice" Jonathon Nicholls.

Sunken Road, Arras. "Cheerful Sacrifice" Jonathon Nicholls.

German prisoners, Arras. "Cheerful Sacrifice" Jonathon Nicholls.

(7 28 55) GD8995/2 350,000 1/17 HWV(M) Forms/B104—80/3

Army Form B. 104—81A.

No. S/17599
(If replying, please quote above No.)

Infantry _____ Record Office,

Perth

21 - 4 - 1917.

SIR OR ~~MADAM~~,

I regret to have to inform you that a report has been received from the War Office to the effect that (No) S/17599 (Rank) Pte (Name) J Stout (Regiment) Seaforth Highrs. has been wounded, and was admitted to 13 General Hospital Boulogne France on the 13 day of April, 1917 The nature of the wound is Severe right knee

I am to express to you the sympathy and regret of the Army Council.

Any further information received in this office as to his condition will be at once notified to you.

Yours faithfully,

W. Grant
for Officer in charge of Records.
Major
No.1 District

IMPORTANT.—Any change of address should be immediately notified to this Office.

Report from the War Office that Pte. James Stout has been wounded.

James, second from left, at the Brook Hospital.
He is wearing the blue clothes of the wounded tommies.

The helmet that saved James's life can be seen on the wall
to the right of the fireplace in the Medical Hall.

James, on his return to Shetland, fooling around on a picnic on Noss, sheep's wool beard and spying through an old wooden fishing float.

James and Nancy in Shetland.

Harriet with Mama outside the back of the Medical Hall, 1911.

Harriet Mainland Stout 1896-1984

The Years Before the War

Harriet Mainland Stout was 18 years old in 1914 when war was declared. She had just completed her education at the Anderson Institute with high grades in all subjects. But she was not as focused on a career as her older sisters. She played tennis and badminton, took part in theatricals produced by her elder sisters, and judging from Charlie's photographs, enjoyed the social life of the town.

She eventually decided on a career in nursing.

Harriet qualified as a Princess Louise nurse.

Harriet Mainland Stout 1896-1984

The War Years

During the war years Harriet Mainland Stout, known affectionately as "Hal", qualified as a Princess Louise Nurse and served as a theatre nurse at the Gilbert Bain Hospital in Lerwick during the latter years of the war. She sewed diligently for Queen Mary's Needlework Guild and helped organise fundraising whist drives, dances, concerts and sales of work for the war effort.

Lerwick was a bustling naval town during the war years, with a promising social life. Harriet and her sisters attended dances and socials in the town hall, and soon many of the naval personnel became firm friends. They were welcomed into family life at the Medical Hall, and appreciated the hospitality of a real home. The girls enjoyed the attention of these handsome naval officers, and invited them to family picnics, tennis, and parties in the Medical Hall. Harriet is photographed visiting Brough Lodge, Fetlar, home of her friend Lieut. Stanley Nicholson, seated on her right. They have been playing golf with her sister Queenie and a member of the merchant navy. I came across several photographs of Harriet and Lieut. Stanley Nicholson out and about in Shetland during the war. We next see Harriet dressed for tennis with the family friend Lieut. Frank Johnson RNVR on the Lerwick tennis green.

With her sister Queenie and brother Charlie, Harriet joined the expeditions to the Isle of Noss. I think she was particularly fond of the spaniel Roy and often looked after him while Charlie was climbing with his friends. On 9th September, 1916, she devoted a page in the Noss visitors' book to "our faithful dog ... Roy!". Harriet/Roy contributed a poem "A' rovin" attributed to Roy Stout. Harriet had a distinctively neat handwriting.

In 1918 Harriet decided she wanted to leave nursing and train as a dental mechanic in London, and joined her sister Margaret at the YWCA in Highbury. After a short time "she was fed up", and decided to go home. However, she was still in London in July, 1919, when the invitations arrived for the garden party at Buckingham Palace. She was one of the three sisters representing Shetland's outstanding wartime contribution to Queen Mary's Needlework Guild. There is a full account of that memorable day by Margaret Stout.

After the war Harriet settled down in the family home and continued her nursing career in Shetland, interrupted with travels to America.

Harriet, like all her sisters, loved the Fair Isle garments which had become fashionable after the war. Ladies in Lerwick sent directly to Fair Isle for these exquisitely patterned garments or purchased them from the first knitwear shops in town. Harriet also purchased Fair Isle garments from her friend Ethel Brown, who was not only the best hairdresser in town, but the designer and knitter of highly original Fair Isle garments. I found several photographs of Harriet wearing a variety of elaborately patterned Fair Isle garments. She must have had a wonderful wardrobe.

After Mr Stout died in 1928, Harriet, with the family's approval, gave up her nursing career in order to look after Mrs Stout and oversee the running of the Medical Hall. This suited Harriet. She loved the gossipy social life in Lerwick; she and Hilda Ganson[1] were known to stay up all night drinking cups of tea and gossiping!

We will never know if the Great War changed life for Harriet. A romance unfulfilled? A friendship lost?

I do know that we all loved Aunt Harriet. As a small girl in Lerwick during the last war, I remember thrilling moonlight walks with her, my hand firmly in hers, along Commercial Street and on towards the Knab, the blackout accentuating the silvery light of the moon on the turbulent water.

---

1   Hilda Ganson a daughter of Mr and Mrs Ganson, a prominent Lerwick family who had built and lived at Brentham Place, Harbour Street, Lerwick. Hilda owned and managed the Ness of Sound dairy and West Hall. She had a first class diploma from the Edinburgh School of Cookery and could have taught domestic science, but preferred her dairy.

Harriet at the wheel of the
SS *Earl* bound for Unst.

Harriet and Lieut. Frank Johnson
RNVR "Johns" enjoying a game of
tennis in Lerwick.

Harriet left, with her sister Anne at the tennis green, 1916.

1916. 1916

Sept. 9th   Harriet M. Stout. Lerwick.
               Lilian M. Spence.   "
               Margaret Manson.   "
               Queenie Stout.   "
Our Ever Faithful Dog —— Roy!   "

A'rovin'

Across Noss Sound we took our way;
    Mark well what I do say!
Across Noss Sound we took our way,
Spending a most delightful day,
Around the island rovin'
    The Lord knows where!

Then down to the sandy bay we went;
    Mark well what I do say!
Then down to the sandy bay we went,
And a joyous time in the sea we spent,
But now we've gone a'rovin'
    The Lord knows where!

                               Roy Stout.

Roy's page in the Noss visitors' book, with assistance from Harriet.

Harriet in the back of an RN lorry, going somewhere?

Harriet visiting Brough Lodge, Fetlar, home of her friend
Lieut. Stanley Nicholson. Queenie and a sailor complete the group.

A family picnic after the war. From left. Young Walter Garriock, Harriet resplendent in Fair Isle cardigan and hat, Queenie sporting a Fair Isle hat, Mr Stout and Nancy wearing a gorgeous Fair Isle cardigan and hat, Bina and Capt. Garrick in the rear.

A family gathering in the Medical Hall dining room 1920s. From left. Mr Stout, Anne Irvine née Stout, Nanny with baby John, Mrs Stout, and Margaret. Seated front, Harriet with young David Irvine. Harriet is wearing a splendid Fair Isle jumper with an exquisite enamel butterfly brooch, a gift from Lieut Levy. She looks so happy.

Charlie took this delightful photograph of
James and Queenie in nautical attire 1906.

Jessie Alexandra Stout 1901-1982

The Years Before the War

Jessie Alexandra Stout was named after Queen Alexandra and soon family and friends were calling her "Queenie", and Queenie she remained for the rest of her life.

As the youngest member of the family, Queenie was spoilt by her elder sisters, but not dominated. They were occupied with their own careers, allowing Queenie space to develop her own interests, quite different from her sisters. She was a keen fisherman, enjoyed tennis and badminton, and later photography and archaeology.

Trolling through pre-war copies of *The Shetland News* we find Queenie Stout taking part in concerts and theatricals in the town often produced and written by her older sisters. She obligingly played the part of the "page boy" on numerous occasions in her sisters' productions.

Queenie fishing on the Loch of Cliff, Unst, 1914.

Cleaning sphagnum moss, Queenie in the centre with Flora Campbell on left and Anne and Margaret to her right.

Jessie Alexandra Stout 1901-1982

The War Years

Queenie Stout was a 13 year old schoolgirl at the start of the war. She lost no time in following in her sisters' footsteps performing in concerts and plays in aid of war funds.

The Shetland News reported on a sale and concert held in the town hall in 1915 in "aid of Belgium". Betty Stout had written a topical, witty and "hamely" sketch in dialect performed by Queenie Stout in "native" costume, to great applause. Almost certainly the same costume previously worn by Margaret Stout. Theatrical costumes were stored in an old seaman's kist for family use. The sheriff, who opened the sale, considered himself a "rare" bird having attended the University of Brussels. The proceeds from the sale were to help "the homeless wretched people, driven from their comfortable homes, strangers in a strange land".

Queenie enjoyed tennis and badminton with her sisters and friends, but fishing was a private affair when she preferred to be on her own. Her skill with boats proved providential when, walking past the Hoversta pier one day, she heard a faint cry, ran to the pier and saw a pale child's face above the water, struggling, and getting into deeper water. Queenie at once got into a boat, rowed off, and managed after some difficulty, to pull the boy out by the collar of his coat. The nine year old boy, who could not swim, recovered on dry land. The account of the rescue appeared in *The Shetland News* but Queenie was very modest about her role in saving the boy's life.

Queenie grew up quickly during the war from a 13-year-old school girl to a young lady of 17 years. She had a self confidence beyond her years, and was soon allowed to attend social events in Lerwick where she met naval personnel, many of whom she must have known through their visits to the Medical Hall. Queenie had a friend in Lieut. Robert Watson RNVR who was a frequent visitor to the Medical Hall. He had been assigned to one of the hydrophone boats which swept the sea with microphones to listen for enemy submarines. There seems to have been a craze for exchanging hats and having your photograph taken by Charlie!

Queenie decided on a career in pharmacy and started her apprenticeship in 1917 in the Medical Hall, completing her qualifications at the University of Glasgow.

After the war Queenie travelled to Europe and America visiting relations and friends. She was a rival photographer to Charlie and her postcards of the Lindberghs in Lerwick were much sought after. She studied archaeology and geology, gave up pharmacy and opened a jewellers shop. She bought a car which made her very popular with the family and faithfully recorded jolly picnics to sandy beaches, among rocky seascapes, or in the heather clad hills.

Queenie grew up quickly during the war years and although she trod her own path, she must have been encouraged to do so by the example of her liberated sisters and enlightened parents.

Queenie and Harriet exploring caves on Bressay

Queenie with Lieut. Watson in the Medical Hall garden. Swapping hats seems to have been all the rage!

Lieut. Watson on board one of the hydrophone boats.

Queenie looking out of the window of her car, her sister Margaret sitting on the running board with her daughter (the author), 1935.

Captain Henry Mainland on board his ship
in the Philippines before the war.

Captain Henry Mainland 1876-1932

The Years Before the War

Captain Henry Mainland, Mrs Stout's youngest brother, had led a colourful life at sea trading between the Philippines and Shanghai in his sailing schooner. In 1909, aged 32, he was made inspector of vessels for the Philippine government with headquarters in Manila, where anyone from the "Old Rock" were guaranteed to receive a hearty welcome.

There was always great excitement when Henry returned to Shetland to visit the family. He came bearing exotic gifts including a green parrot named Loretto in a big brass cage, who lived with the family for nearly fifty years! A set of Javanese Gamalan drums, (a member of the family spotted a similar set in Osborne House, a gift to Queen Victoria) giant sea shells, exquisitely crafted straw work, and beautifully hand embroidered blouses from the Philippines. Bananas were displayed exotically in fruit bowls and consumed all too quickly. Henry gave one to the housemaid who placed it carefully in her trunk as a keepsake. She was found in tears some weeks later clutching a very rotten black banana.

Henry was a great favourite with the Stout girls who regarded him more as a brother than an uncle. His chief officer, a Spaniard, became Margaret's pen friend. He wrote to her on colourful postcards to improve his English.

By 1914 Capt. Henry Mainland had become an American citizen, married his Shetland cousin Mary Sinclair from Ollaberry, in New York, and now commanded an American ship the SS *Lanco*.

Captain Henry Mainland.

Captain Henry Mainland 1876-1932

The War Years

Headline. SS *Lanco* sunk by German submarine, 1916.

Captain Henry Mainland, the officers and crew of the American SS *Lanco* were lucky to have survived after their ship was sunk by a German submarine on 2nd November, 1916, off the coast of Portugal.

Captain Mainland was on his way to Britain with a cargo of rice when, in the dark, they were hailed by a German submarine which fired shots across their bow. The chief officer, a Spaniard, was sent to board the submarine, and returned with the order to leave their vessel. The account continues from the diary of Margaret Stout.

> Uncle Henry was an American citizen and his ship was American. They were taken on board the German submarine. Uncle Henry was climbing up the ladder to board the submarine carrying a small leather case with all his personal papers, money, photographs and his own treasures. He handed his case to a German officer at the top, as he needed both hands to climb on board, when he set foot on the submarine he turned to the officer and said, "My case please". The officer looked blank and said, "What case?" and so Uncle Henry lost all his personal possessions and papers.

Captain Mainland continues:

> A German lieutenant and several crew members boarded the SS *Lanco*, ransacked my cabin, even taking the picture frames from the walls, including nice Japanese frames containing photos of the Stout girls. They placed a bomb in the engine room and blew her up.

> The commander of the submarine was anxious to off-load his passengers as quickly as possible, and sighting a ship he thought was Spanish, gave chase. It was

not until he came alongside that he realised that the ship was Norwegian, but he had no option other than to transfer Captain Mainland and crew to Captain Johnsen of the *Tromp*.

Captain Mainland takes up the story:

> We were well treated on board the Norwegian ship, and Captain Johnsen shared and shared alike. He claims that it was us that saved him, as he had been held up earlier in the day, and the German submarine had been so busy that they had not time to attend to him. When it got dark he was making best his escape when we overtook him in the submarine, and he thought when he saw the submarine he was doomed also. He was surprised when we were hustled aboard. The submarine left in a great hurry as vessel lights had been seen and he feared that torpedo boats might be after him.

The *Tromp* eventually docked safely at Port of Barry Docks on the north shore of the Bristol Channel. Later in the war German submarines sank ships with all hands, so Captain Mainland and his crew were very lucky.

The sinking of a neutral American ship by a German submarine became a diplomatic incident. Questions of ownership and neutrality were asked and were still unresolved when America entered the war.

As an American citizen Capt. Mainland was well treated and reimbursed by the American consulate, who granted him leave to visit the family in Shetland, although he had to report to the police daily.

The Stout girls were left wondering if their photographs now adorned the quarters of a German submarine!

Family picnic before the war. From left. Roy, Mr Stout, Mrs Stout, Capt. Henry Mainland, Betty, Margaret, Harriet and Alice Mainland.

Loretto, the Medical Hall parrot, a gift from Capt. Mainland.

Private James Johnston.
Canadian Expeditionary Force, on leave in Shetland.

The Cousins Who Went to War

From the middle of the 19th century hundreds of Shetlanders had emigrated to the New World and now the next generation were enlisting to fight for the "old country." Members of both Mr and Mrs Stout's families emigrated to Australia, New Zealand and Canada, but letters ensured that family ties were not lost. The young cousins who came to France made their way to Shetland to spend their leave, those who had been drafted to Gallipoli were not so lucky.

Private James Johnston's mother was the widowed sister of Mr Stout. His elder brother had already spent ten years under the patronage of Mr Stout and now had his own chemist shop in Glasgow.

Now it was James's turn to be welcomed into the Stout family while he attended the Anderson Educational Institute for five years and then embarked on a career in the civil service. He emigrated to Canada, but as soon as war was declared he enlisted with the Canadian 7th Battalion and set sail for France. He was twice wounded, in 1916 at Mouguet's farm on the Somme, and at Arras in 1918. He spent his leaves in Shetland and his letter describing the giant mine detonated by "Fritz" was printed in *The Shetland Times*.

Private James Johnston. Canadian Expeditionary Force 1914 – 1918. Writing from somewhere in France to a relative at the Medical Hall Lerwick. 2nd September, 1916:

> Here we are again back for a few more days rest. I will endeavour to give you an account of my experiences this last trip which should prove interesting and I certainly found it so myself. We went up several days ago and took up our position in some trenches to the right of the last place we were in. These trenches have a very unsavoury reputation and are a place where Fritz is very liberal in sending over trench mortars, sausage, minenwerfers and fish-tails – a very formidable quartet. They are fired from a very simple weapon (used centuries ago, I think) and their range is not much more than 100 yards. The dugout is no protection against them.
>
> The first few days were pretty quiet (?) although we sampled his assortment, we

only had a few casualties. I was out on listening duty one night, which was uneventful, although he kept sweeping our parapet with his machine gun and sniping was pretty brisk. We had a little hole, and by crouching pretty low when the machine gun was coming our way, we were safe enough, although several rifle grenades landed pretty close.

One night – the most interesting – we were all packed up ready and had about three hours to wait, when our commander got information that Fritz was going to blow up a mine. So my platoon was sent down to a support trench to be ready when the mine went up to rush to the crater. The rest of the battalion had likewise different positions and aims. Well, we waited, and there was some talk of its not going up that night, but we had to stay here till the other battalion relieved us anyway. It had become pretty dark by now and was rather ominously quiet. I remember the fellow next to me saying so, and that he didn't like it – poor chap, he got killed too, shortly after, – when suddenly there was a dull roar and the earth began to shake. There was a second explosion a few seconds after the first, and looking up I saw tons of earth and a cloud of fire high up in the sky and our trench rocked just like a boat on a rough day. It seemed to me that we were going to be enveloped at first, and a lot of earth fell around us, but we were all right as far as the mine was concerned.

Fritz opened up with his artillery the second the mine went up, but ours were only a few seconds behind him, and gave him better than he gave us. Then our Captain gave us the order to get up to the front line, as, of course, we expected Fritz to come over and it was too dark to see. Well, we got up there in double quick time, whilst Fritz was shelling our supports all the time. We were all supplied with a stock of bombs and for a while we were pulling pins and throwing bombs at intervals, and others of us were firing over to Fritz's trenches. Meantime our number one company went over and got possession of the crater. I think we gave Fritz a pretty good surprise when we got on the job so soon, and if he had ever tried to come over, he would have had a great reception.

Things quietened down after a time, and we continued to stand to on the fire slop, shooting at regular intervals over Fritz's parapet, whilst the company that were in the crater "consolidated their position". I thought that we would not get relieved that night and would have to wait till next, but at last word came to scabbard our bayonets and move out as the relieving force were in. We were soon on our way back. Throughout the night I threw over about twenty bombs and fired pretty close to 200 rounds of ammunition, so I was pretty tired and was mighty glad to get back for a decent sleep. Our fellows behaved fine during all this time, and Fritz was pretty lucky in staying in his own trenches, as he would have got a reception that he wouldn't have forgot in a hurry.

For my own part, I felt good and was not in the least bit excited or alarmed after the mine incident closed, and we got bust doing something. It seems to key a fellow up somehow when there is something on, and according to my idea the worst time is when you are lying inactive during a bombardment, as I was in my first trip up the line some time ago. To give you an idea of the shock of the mine when it went up, one of the sergeants told me it was about 125 yards long by 75 yards wide, and about 80 feet deep. Quite a small sized hole, eh! It was an experience I am not sorry for seeing, but I must say I don't want to be so close to one again, nor would anyone else I imagine, what! We had a very small casualty list considering the operation, and I think that Fritz was cut up pretty bad by our artillery and got off a good deal worse than we did.

Well we are back to our football and cricket and picture shows, and will be ready to go up pretty soon again. So you see a fellow soon gets used to everything and just takes things as they come.

On 10th September, 1916, Pte. James Johnston was wounded when his battalion went into action in the Somme district. He wrote an account of the action from a military hospital in England, which was also printed in *The Shetland Times*.

SHETLANDER WOUNDED IN ACTION

We went into action in the Somme district on the night of the 7th instant, relieving the Australians there. We were bombed until the 10th when I got hit and got out of it.

We were on a ridge and the Germans were on two other ridges. We had taken their front trench, and in front, about 150 yards, we had about 14 stretcher cases in an advanced dressing station between us and Fritz, and down here it's a custom for us to go out under the white flag to bring in our wounded. (Fritz uses red.)

Well, the first party that went out a shell landed among them and killed six and wounded four. I went out with the second party and we got out alright. But what a road! From our battalion dressing station to the stretcher cases was about 300 yards, and the ground looked as if it had been ploughed on a large scale. Shell hole overlaps shell hole. Fritz dropped some shells pretty close around us, but we made that trip alright and went out again, but we had hardly got more than 50 yards on our way back. I changed off the stretcher and was carrying the flag when – biff! A whizz-bang hit me a glancing blow on the left thigh making a flesh wound about the size of a six inch circle – didn't hit a bone though. The shell exploded about 30 yards further on after it hit me, but I was the only victim.

A whizz-bang is about an 18lb shell and is about the fastest shell they throw. It is fired almost straight from the gun, so you can know how lucky I was, and this wound will heal up all right in due time without disabling me at all. I have to lie on my right side all the time, and I can't sit up, but otherwise I am all right. There are three of us in this ward who stay in bed. The rest are all in pretty good condition, and certainly make some row.

James Johnston returned to Vancouver and his career in the civil service, married happily, and enjoyed visits from members of the family. His great passion was fishing.

Mrs Stout's uncle Henry Mainland who had emigrated to Australia, lost his only son. *The Shetland Times* reported the death:

> SHETLANDER KILLED IN ACTION
> Private Henry Owen Mainland
> We regret to have to announce the death of Private Henry Owen Mainland of the Australian Expeditionary Force. Private Mainland was killed in action in Belgium on the 17th October 1917 after having seen some hard fighting. He joined the Australians some time back and came over to complete his training in England. In due course he was drafted to France where he was wounded in action. After recovering in a French hospital, he was sent to the battlefront again where he met his death gallantly.
> Private Mainland was the only son of Henry Mainland of Sharks Bay, West Australia, where he was the owner of a prosperous Pearl Fishing Station and a fleet of luggers. Mr Mainland who is 77 years of age was about to retire and hand the business over to his only son, who was not among the youngest of men, but had decided that his countries call was very clear.

The family were very distressed at the news of the death of Henry Mainland, particularly Margaret, who had written to his father on Sunday afternoons at the behest of Mama. Mrs Stout was deeply grieved that Henry had not had leave to visit the family in Shetland.

From Mrs Stout's side of the family several members from West Australia joined the Australian Expeditionary Force, Lance Corporal Clarence Sinclair, Lance Corporal Jack Sinclair and Trooper Malcolm Sinclair of the 10th Australian Light Horse. From New Zealand, 2nd Lieut. Jack Sinclair 24th Reinforcements New Zealand Expeditionary Force was killed in action on 27th March, 1918. The family, who had been expecting him to visit Shetland on leave were "all very cut up about it".

Lance Corporal Jack Sinclair from West Australia came to London on leave where he met his cousin Margaret Stout, who also had leave and was returning home. Jack was planning to visit the family in Shetland so they decided to travel together.

Charlie photographed them both out and about in Shetland, Jack in breeches and sloughed hat. He was handsome and caused hearts to flutter.

Mrs Stout's nephew Joseph Strathern from Edderton, Scotland, where the Stout siblings had spent holidays, enlisted as an Air Mechanic 3rd class, in the Royal Flying Corps in January 1918. He clearly showed promise, because he became a Flight Cadet in July 1918, and in April 1919 he was moved to Kinross where he was appointed Honorary 2nd Lieutenant which suggests his training was complete, but now the war was over.

Three of Mr Stout's brothers emigrated to Queensland, Australia, in 1876. Three of their sons enlisted with the Australian Imperial Forces, (A.I.F.) Pte. Henry Stout and Pte. George Stout were both wounded in France, but made good recoveries and returned to Australia. Pte. Victor Harold Stout embarked on the *Clan MacGillivray* in Brisbane for Gallipoli where he fought during the campaign, 25th April-20th December, 1915. One of the soldiers in the photograph of a trench at Gallipoli is Victor. Following the evacuation from Gallipoli the AIF was reorganised in Egypt, before being moved to northern France, and the carnage of the battle of the Somme.

The battalion then moved to Mouquet Farm, in the Ypres salient, fought a major battle around Bullecourt with horrendous casualties and finally remained in the Ypres sector fighting around Polygon Wood during the 3rd battle of Ypres. Victor was very lucky to survive and return to Australia, unfortunately by then suffering from the dreaded influenza.

Herbert Erland Fordyce Clark was born in Edinburgh but both his parents were born in Unst, Shetland. His father was related to Mr Charles B. Stout, who also you may remember, came from Unst. Herbert joined the Lothian and Border Horse in 1914, gained a commission as a second lieutenant in the 4th battalion Royal Scots in 1916, and was wounded in France in January 1918. By March 1918 we find Herbert attached as a lieutenant to the Royal Flying Corps, which became the Royal Air Force on 1st April, 1918. Sadly, by the end of the war he was judged unfit for flying, only fit for ground duties, a consequence of his wound in 1918.

Nearer to home Lieut. Thomas Stout of the 8th Scottish Rifles was killed in action at the Dardanelles on the 28th June, 1918. Sergeant Webster Irvine of the Pals Battalion Liverpool was reported missing in the battle of Verdun in August 1915 aged 31 years and Private James Stout of the Seaforth Highlanders, son of Mr and Mrs C.B. Stout was wounded at the battle of Arras in April 1917.

The large families of the time ensured that practically everyone had a relative at war.

Six members of the Australian Expeditionary Force in a trench at Gallipoli. One of them is Victor Harold Stout. From the right: The first soldier is wearing an arm band denoting Stretcher Bearer and a Turkish cap. The second is holding a "gong" to be struck to warn of an attack, a piece of "trench art". The third may be wearing a Turkish cap and the fourth is wearing a Topee, his identity disc on view and holding official looking papers. The soldier behind is pulling on a Turkish cap and beside him a soldier is flourishing his bayonet.

Lieut. Herbert E. Fordyce Clark in 1914 with the Lothian & Border Horse.

Pte. Henry O. Mainland killed in action 17th October, 1917.

A Gallipoli Campaign Centenary Commemoration Certificate in the name of Victor Harold Stout.

Grave of Pte Henry O. Mainland, New British Cemetery, Dochy Farm, Belgium. Australian Infantry killed in action 17th October, 1917 Ypres Flanders, Belgium.

The dairy boat from Bressay arriving at the South End, Lerwick.

Appendix

A Little of What the Family Did Next

Mrs Anne Irvine (née Stout)

Married life for Anne had begun in Hankow, China. She found herself presiding over a large establishment teeming with Chinese servants, fortunately for Anne the chief house boy organised the smooth running of the household.

Anne was devoted to her first baby, David, and had time for little else. She discovered that the Amah, who had been engaged as a nanny, had left her young son with her parents so she could work. Anne was horrified and instructed Amah to send for her son who could assist his mother. In due course the little boy arrived. The next day the courtyard behind the house was teeming with house servants, wives and children, all shouting that they wanted their wives and children to live at the house too. Mr Irvine had to take a firm stand and send them all packing before the idea spread to other households in the concession. Anne, however, refused to send Amah's son away and he became David's "boy" and carried his toys around on a silk cushion. Amah had "Lotus feet"[1] and Anne was terrified that she would fall carrying the baby down flights of stairs, but she never faltered.

Anne and young David returned to Shetland, her husband following at a later date. She made her home at 91 King Harald Street, and David was joined by John, Margaret and Fredrick. She was a member of the Zetland Education Committee and an active member of the Scottish Women's Rural Institute. She continued to write and lecture, now on life and customs in China.

---

[1] "Lotus Feet", described the custom of binding the feet of very young girls to modiy the shape and size of the foot. Small feet were considered a status symbol essential in making a good marriage. The ideal length for a bound foot was 4 inches or 10 cm. Just the front of the little shoe protruded from wide bottomed trousers. Foot binding was extremely painful and often led to horrific deformity.

During the Second World War she was an ARP warden (Air Raid Precautions warden). If the siren sounded she donned her tin hat and went to her first aid post, leaving the house and children in charge of the maid. She was keen to take the children away from the town during the summer, and teemed up with her sister Margaret and her children to rent Ordale House in Unst. We loved it. The large kitchen with flagged floor, vast black range, huge kitchen table and dresser glittering with old china. Every morning we trooped off to the beach, where there was a cave large enough to hold us six children. At the sound of an aircraft we were ushered into the cave and Anne donned her tin hat and stood silhouetted in the entrance until the suspect danger had passed. This was a sensible precaution after two lighthouse stations had been machine gunned by enemy aircraft and people killed.

Anne cared deeply for her children and actively encouraged them in imaginative and constructive play. Elaborate Meccano constructions were built at the weekends for model railways and did not have to be dismantled until Sunday night. Monopoly games lasted for days and everyone played Mahjong with sets brought home from China.

For a short time I stayed with Aunt Annie while attending the Central School. I can see her now warming our coats one by one as we left for school in the morning. As the youngest, I was in awe of my clever creative cousins who tolerated me with great good humour. I treasure the time I spent at 91 King Harold Street and loved Aunt Annie who had made me so welcome.

Mrs Elizabeth Brown Levy (née Stout)

After her marriage to Lieut. Nathan Levy of the American navy in Paris in 1919, Betty made her home in America. She and her two sons Charles and Rolf made frequent visits to Europe and Shetland where she once stayed for two years. During the Second World War she took long holidays in Mexico and sent us children magic parcels of Mexician handmade toys and ceramics. She confronted British Customs and Excise with parcels for starving relatives and we were introduced to " jello, spam and cornmeal".

Betty attended a ceramics class in her home town for many years, and spent her time and considerable talent making imaginative and decorative objects based on Shetland folklore, which she sent as gifts to family and friends. Her thoughts were always with Shetland.

Appendix – A Little of What the Family Did Next

Charles Brown Stout MPS

Charlie led a charmed life in the years between the wars, judging by the photographic albums crammed with pictures of jolly groups of chums out motoring, picnicking, camping, sailing, swimming, climbing, fishing and shooting. He travelled continually to Norway and Holland often by fishing boats, to visit friends and sometimes to do a spot of business. He was very hospitable and kept open house to all his friends in Shetland and visiting friends from Norway and Holland. He organised his life to have time for his social activities and still manage two successful pharmacies.

Before the National Health Scheme, if you needed minor medical attention, you headed for the pharmacist who treated you to the best of his ability. The shop was always busy, administering not only to the local population, but also to the huge cosmopolitan population that descended on Lerwick during the fishing season.

Charlie was a clever chemist and during the Second World War made all sorts of hair and beauty products which were unobtainable, for sale in the shop. The local girls wanted to look their best with 20,000 servicemen stationed on the islands.

He kept open house to the Norwegian members of the Shetland Bus, and entertained them royally. Sometimes they were able to deliver notes and cigarettes to his friends in Norway. I know he was longing to go with them.

I have a silver coffee pot inscribed "Chorley's special prize" which came into my possession after he died. The Norwegians called him "Chorley" and this coffee pot was presented to him at a special gathering at his house just before the war ended. The inscription relates to a private jest!

I think this is the moment to leave Charlie entertaining the brave Norwegian resistance fighters, helping to free his beloved Norway.

Mrs Margaret Bannatyne Dennis (née Stout)

After the war, Margaret travelled to America with her sister Betty and her American husband, who had arranged a few days sightseeing for them in New York, before heading for Philadelphia and home. Margaret and Betty caused a sensation ! They were both wearing Fair Isle cardigans! People jostled them to get a closer look and ask them where they had come from. Cameras appeared and Nat, somewhat bewildered, hurried them into an hotel for lunch.

Margaret knew that she could only stay three years in America and retain her British nationality, so there was no time to lose.

She was successful in obtaining a teaching post at a progressive girl's boarding school with an international staff. The school had been founded by an American philanthropist and built in the style of an English arts and crafts village. Margaret lived with another teacher and ten girls in Red Gables, house mother and domestic science teacher to the school. Carson College was an orphanage unlike any other.

Betty had spotted an advertisement for a companion and tutor to a young lady and thought that this would be an opportunity for Margaret to experience another way of life in America. Margaret was chosen from dozens of applicants for her knowledge of Latin from schooldays at the Anderson Educational Institute.

The family lived in a Spanish style mansion with galleried rooms brought from ancient castles in Spain, surrounded by ornate Italian gardens, a tennis court and a swimming pool. Margaret and her charge attended lectures, concerts and exhibitions, and spent the summer holidays at Buck Hill Falls, an exclusive holiday camp where Margaret learnt to swim and play tennis.

Three years had flown by and Margaret was making plans to continue her journey around the world and join her sister Anne in China. Her employers had been exceedingly generous and considerate and were devastated, but understood when Margaret explained her reason for leaving.

She travelled west across America to Vancouver, breaking her journey to spend a week in Yellowstone Park. In Vancouver she stayed with her Aunt Lilly and Uncle Tom Stout, who was the proprietor of a chemist shop.

Margaret continued her journey to Victoria to join the President Grant to sail across the Pacific to China. Margaret writes:

> I had booked one of the less expensive cabins to share with another girl who was going to join her father, a missionary, in Manilla. The purser a handsome young man said " Oh, you girls can't remain here. I will move you to a deck cabin, the ship is only half full". We had a very jolly crossing dancing on the deck every other night with fellows from the Deep South travelling to China to oversee tobacco plantations.
>
> Our first port of call was Yokohoma. Two of the "tobacco boys" said they would like to take us for a Japanese meal in Tokyo, a short rail journey away. Off we went. The Japanese restaurant was perched on top of a hill, the beautiful flower garden was lit with lanterns, and tame monkeys chattered among the trees. Inside we were taken to a room with bamboo walls, wood floor and sat on cushions at a low table.

Appendix – A Little of What the Family Did Next

A Japanese girl clad in a kimono flitted silently in and out with an amazing array of delicious dishes. We had Samsu in tiny heated cups. We had a lot of fun and got safely back to the ship not too late!

Shanghai at last! The "tobacco boys" again asked us ashore to dinner. I had long cherished an elaborate Menu from the Aster House Hotel, Shanghai, given to me by Uncle Henry in Shetland! So off we went. We had a lovely meal and much fun.

After dinner the boys took us for a taxi ride all round Shanghai and back to the ship where we said our goodbyes. They had been good companions and treated us very correctly.

Margaret stayed with friends in Shanghai who escorted her to the river boat for Kiukaing where she was to meet John Irvine, her brother in Law. Before leaving Shanghai she had a surprise visit and dinner with Pat Macdougal, a Shetland friend who was with the Hong Kong and Shanghai Bank. "It seemed so funny seeing Pat Macdougal in Shanghai, such a wild boy." The "wild boy" had served in the Royal Flying Corps during the war as a lieutenant, and was posted to 24 squadron RFC flying single seater fighters. He was twice wounded but his tally of seven victories and ace status won him the Military Cross which was presented to him by King George V at Buckingham Palace on the 10th May, 1918.

John was waiting for Margaret at Kiukiang with chairs to carry them up the mountain to Kuling and Anne. Kuling was a summer settlement in the hills where Europeans came to escape the stifling heat of the plains. It was now evening and Anne was out with a lamp to greet the travellers. It must have been a great reunion!

Life was very pleasant in Kuling. Several of the Chinese servants had accompanied Anne from their house in Hankow, including Amah to look after baby David. The social life of the plains continued and days were devoted to tennis, afternoon teas and mah-jong, dinner parties and bridge. Chinese pedlars came regularly to the house with exquisite embroidery, lacquer work and jade jewellery.

Summer over everyone returned to their houses in Hankow. The Chinese indoor staff could only imagine that Margaret was John's second wife, and was always referred to her Missy Number Two! Anne would not leave David for any length of time and asked Margaret to accompany John to a grand Chinese wedding. Margaret was the only woman there except for the tiny bride in dark glasses standing all through the sumptuous feast on her tiny bound feet, never a morsel passing her lips. Margaret wrote a memorable account of this lavish and now unique celebration, which was published in the first edition of the Anderson Educational Institute magazine (A.E.I.) in 1926.

There was always trouble beyond Hankow where the railway and European influence ended. The men in the concessions volunteered for military training and were all armed. John eventually decided that Anne and David should return to Britain with Margaret who could help Anne look after David on the long sea voyage. Margaret had met a gentleman on the golf course who had just won the Hankow Golf Club Challenge Cup. They exchanged addresses.

Margaret left the ship at the start of the Suez Canal and with a few other intrepid passengers rode on camels through the desert to the pyramids and the Sphinx, rejoining the ship at Suez.

When the ship docked at Southampton Anne and Margaret had one thought in mind. Shetland and home.

The first Scottish Women's Rural Institutes (SWRI) had been established and the idea was spreading across Scotland. Margaret applied and secured the post of area organiser for the northeast of Scotland, with an office in Aberdeen. Two years later the long awaited-post of domestic science teacher in Lerwick became vacant. Margaret immediately applied and was successful. She spent her spare time researching vegetable dyes and learning to spin and make Shetland taatit rugs.

Since leaving China she and the gentleman she had met on the golf course had corresponded. It was 1930 and he was planning to retire to the south of England. Margaret eventually travelled to Kent where they had a joyous reunion, announced their engagement and plans to marry in Shetland.

The wedding drew family and friends together for a memorable celebration. Charlie took a cine film of the happy couple leaving St Olaf's Church and posing for photographs in a nearby garden. Mr and Mrs Richard Dennis took a motoring honeymoon through Scotland to Kent where they had purchased a large property in the country. Friends and relations came to visit and stay, Shetlanders enjoyed the prolific fruit orchards and Margaret's homemade jams. She joined the Meopham WRI and lectured on Shetland Life and Shetland Arts and Crafts to WRI throughout the south of England. It was an idyllic life until the outbreak of the Second World War.

After a lone Nazi plane dropped a bomb on the property in 1940, Richard and Margaret decided that the south of England was not the place to be, especially as they now had two young children. Margaret set off to stay first in London, then Suffolk and Edinburgh and finally she just wanted to go home to Shetland.

She arrived in Shetland with her two children after an eventful journey. The small plane, a de Havilland Dragon Rapide, crashed on take off in Orkney. Margaret suffered an eye injury but luckily a Harley Street eye surgeon was stationed in Orkney attached to the navy, and he was able to save her sight. She and the two children had to spend a week in Kirkwall Hospital where the children were spoilt with gifts from wartime charities! Margaret eventually flew on to Shetland in a small naval plane to the comfort and support of her family.

Appendix – A Little of What the Family Did Next

Margaret and the children quickly settled into life in wartime Shetland. She lived between the Medical Hall and Charlie's holiday cottage at Sound, until twice the peace was shattered by mines exploding on the beach below the cottage. She continued to give her Make Do and Mend classes, that she had started in Kent, to the SWRI.

After two years in Shetland, Margaret and Richard decided that as the German invasion had never happened and the Blitz was over, it was safe to return to Kent. No sooner had they arrived than the doodle bugs also arrived – their flight path was across Kent. It was a terrifying time and the family slept in their Anderson Shelter. Soon flights of bombers signalled D-Day and the end of hostilities.

Mr James Stout

James, due to his war disability, had to give up all thoughts of becoming a sports master and continued his banking career in Dunfermline. He came to Shetland for summer holidays with Nancy and their two girls, Kathleen and Dorothy. Charlie took photographs of Jimmy and the girls clowning around on the beach, he must have been great fun to have as a dad!

Miss Harriet Stout

Between the wars Harriet would arrange to rent a schoolhouse in the country during the summer school holidays, and take her mother to enjoy the fresh air and visit old friends. They both enjoyed these holidays enormously and returned to Lerwick refreshed.

During the Second World War, Shetland was awash with servicemen and Harriet and Mrs Stout found themselves again welcoming cousins from overseas. Mrs Stout particularly enjoyed meeting the next generation.

The blackout was rigorously enforced, especially as the Medical Hall was so near the principal pier and shipping. Apparently Harriet had continually allowed a light to shine out from the bathroom and the exasperated warden threatened to "shoot it out if he saw it again". I imagined the scene, Aunt Harriet in the bath, a shot rings out, glass shatters, and screams from Aunt Harriet – but of course it never happened. She was very careful now.

The war over, Harriet made her home in Edinburgh, and with a Shetland friend Hilda Fordyce Clark[2] opened a shop in Hanover Street called the "Spinning Wheel." They sold Shetland knitwear, which neither of them knew much about except that they loved it and always wore it. They enjoyed the cosy atmosphere of the shop with lots of Shetland visitors, and cups of tea. It couldn't last.

Harriet then set off on a world tour with another Shetland friend, Mrs Dr Willie Irvine from Gulberwick. She resumed her nursing career in New Zealand where she visited several relatives including the daughters of Sir Robert Stout who was a second cousin to her father. Robert Stout, schoolmaster, had emigrated to Dunedin, New Zealand in 1863. He became a lawyer and liberal politician and with his wife championed woman's suffrage. Between 1884 and 1930 he was twice elected prime minister and for a considerable time was lord chief justice of New Zealand. "Philosophy and theory triumph over political expediency" was his war cry!

Life was never dull for Harriet.

Mrs Queenie MacWhirter (née Stout)

Queenie married Magnus MacWhirter, an accountant, in Shetland and they had one son Peter. After Mrs Stout died in 1946 they made the Medical Hall their home. Queenie moved the jewellery business to the chemist shop, which was now empty, Charlie having moved to larger premises next door. Queenie pursued her interest in archaeology, geology and photography with visits to Scandinavia. She was a fund of information on family history and genealogy and corresponded with second and third generation cousins in Australia, New Zealand and America. But, she may always be remembered for her escapade with the steamer.[3]

Seeing friends off on the steamer was a relaxed affair, you could sit and chat in their cabin until the second bell and then make a dash for the gangway. Queenie and her friends were so busy talking that they didn't hear the bell! Magnus was

---

2   Hilda Fordyce Clark was sister to Bertie Fordyce Clark. First World War.
3   The boat plying between Aberdeen and Lerwick Shetland was always referred to as the "steamer".

Appendix – A Little of What the Family Did Next

watching the departure of the steamer from the drawing room windows of the Medical Hall. The gangway was pulled up and the steamer set off for Aberdeen. Suddenly she stopped, reversed back to pier, gangway lowered and a small figure was seen scurrying ashore to ribald laughter and cheering. When Queenie returned to the Medical Hall Magnus told her that some idiot had been carried off and the steamer had had to return to the pier! Queenie never said a word.

Bibliography

Banning, Jeremy & Holmes, Richard, *The Battlefields of the First World War*. Published by Constable London, 2013.

Nicholls, Jonathan, *Cheerful Sacrifice*, Published by Leo Cooper, London, 1990.

Martin, Simon, *The Other Titanic*, The Shetland Times Ltd, Lerwick, 2004.

Riddell, Linda K., *Shetland and the Great War*, The Shetland Times Ltd, Lerwick, 2015.

The Shetland News

The Shetland Times

About the Author

Margaret Stuart is the daughter of Margaret Stout of the Medical Hall, Lerwick, Shetland. She has happy memories of her early school days at the Infant and Central School in Lerwick leading to grammar school and a four year degree course at the Royal College of Art, London (School of Painting). She exhibited annually at the Royal Academy in London.

Margaret returned to Shetland in 1968 and lived at Burrastow House near Walls. She inherited the family passion for Shetland's history, crafts and culture and established "Shetland from Shetland" the internationally successful knitwear company. For eight years Margaret curated many memorable exhibitions for the Shetland Textile Museum at the Weisdale Mill.

Her extensive collections of artefacts were organised into a museum of Shetland Life and Shetland Textile Museum at her property in Walls, where visitors enjoyed the informal, intimate atmosphere.

With the commemorations for the First World War that began in 2014, Margaret was curious to discover what exactly her family's role had been; this book is the result of that research.